In the Saddle with Stuart

The Story of Frank Smith Robertson of Jeb Stuart's Staff

by his grandson
Frank Robertson Reade
with notes, sketches, and maps by
Dr. L. Minor Blackford

edited and with additional notes by
Robert J. Trout

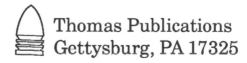

Thomas Publications
Gettysburg, PA 17325

Publisher — Cataloging-in-Publication Data
Robertson, Frank Smith
      In the saddle with Stuart: the story of Frank Smith Robertson of Jeb Stuart's
staff / Condensed, edited, and annotated by Robert J. Trout
      168 pp.   36 x 64.5 cm.
      Includes index, bibliography.
      ISBN 1-57747-029-X
      1. Confederate States of America—History.   2. United States—History—
Civil War, 1861-65—personal narrattives, Confederate.   3. Robertson, Frank
Smith—diaries. I. Title
E470 .R724   973.782   LCC 98-84333

Printed and bound in the United States of America

Published by THOMAS PUBLICATIONS
                  P.O. Box 3031
                  Gettysburg, Pa. 17325

Cover design by Ryan C. Stouch

Cover illustration "Confederate Autumn," courtesy
of Dale Gallon, Gallon Historical Art, 9 Steinwehr
Ave, Gettysburg, PA.

To
Captain James Coleman Molley, Jr.
United States Marine Corps, Distinguished Flying Cross.
Grandson of Captain Frank Smith Robertson, Confederate
States Cavalry, this book was affectionately dedicated by
another and older Grandson.

Contents

Editor's Foreword

The story of how *In the Saddle with Stuart* made the transition from manuscript to finished book is worthy of some comment. Having developed an interest in the staff officers of Maj. Gen. J.E.B. Stuart, I spent several years tracing the lives of the men who made up the staff. In 1988 during a research trip to the University of Virginia, Frank Robertson Reade's unfinished manuscript about his grandfather's war experiences came to my attention. The over two hundred page document was obviously not in a final form, but I felt that it contained valuable material and that the manuscript could be prepared for possible publication at some future time.

Four years later while corresponding with a descendant of the Blackford family, Dr. L. Minor Blackford's version of the manuscript was obtained. He had essentially completed the manuscript as envisioned by Reade, adding material which had been in Reade's notes and an introduction explaining his role. Copies of Frank S. Robertson's letters and a copy of one of his memoirs were also acquired during the same period. It was from these sources that the final manuscript was compiled.

The major difference between Reade's and Blackford's manuscripts and what appears in this book is in the format. In several places Reade jumped back and forth between Robertson's letters and memoirs causing confusion. To eliminate this problem the letters have been separated from the memoirs and presented separately. While some repetition occurs both sources contribute to a better understanding of the events and individuals being discussed.

Reade also had a tendency to break up the memoirs and the letters with his own comments and observations. Many of these were informative, but they made what Robertson actually wrote difficult to follow. Blackford did not alter these passages and in completing the manuscript maintained Reade's style. Since the main focus was to be on Robertson's experiences most of Reade's statements have been moved to footnotes, rearranged within the text, or in a few instances eliminated, as they were comments of a personal nature directed at family.

In some places Reade quoted from other works (i.e. Freeman's *Lee's Lieutenants* or McClellan's *I Rode with Jeb Stuart*). Those passages that were an integral part of the narrative or the footnote have been retained, but a few that did not contribute to a better understanding of the text were deleted.

In their footnotes Reade and Blackford attempted to provide additional information about events and people mentioned by Robertson. Here, too, some editing has been done, mostly in simplifying the wording or eliminating a personal comment. Where necessary other footnotes have been added (signified by [Ed.]).

Finally the last three chapters of Dr. L. Minor Blackford's manuscript contained a significant amount of material which did not specifically concern Robertson. These chapters have been condensed and only what pertained directly to Robertson has been presented.

Robert J. Trout
Myerstown
May 1993

Editor's Acknowledgements

The assistance of numerous individuals and institutions in preparing this book for publication is gratefully acknowledged. Special thanks goes to Mrs. Sally-Bruce Blackford McClatchey and her husband, Mr. Marvin R. McClatchey, who not only provided a copy of Dr. L. Minor Blackford's manuscript but also contributed the sketches he prepared for Reade's manuscript; Mr. Jonathan Walters of the University of Chicago Library for providing and granting permission to publish letters from the Wyndham Robertson Papers; Mr. Ervin L. Jordan, Jr., and Mr. Michael Plunkett of the University of Virginia Library who assisted in obtaining and granted permission to use Frank R. Reade's manuscript; Mr. L. C. Angle and The Historical Society of Washington County, Virginia, for providing a copy of Frank S. Robertson's memoirs; Mr. James S. Patton of "Gay Mont," who furnished additional information on Frank S. Robertson; Miss Jennifer Young, who offered her valuable time, hospitality, and advice on numerous occasions; Mr. Scott Mauger, for his advice and encouragement; Robert E. Lee Trout, my son, who spent hours typing on the computer; and finally to my wife, Judy, for her patience and understanding.

Capt. Frank Smith Robertson, assistant engineer officer to Maj. Gen. J. E. B. Stuart from March 1863 to May 12, 1864.

Foreword

In the summer of 1860 Frank Smith Robertson invited his college chum, Eugene Blackford, to spend some weeks with him at his home in the mountains of southwest Virginia. These nineteen-year-old boys occupied a garret where they could make as much noise as they pleased without disturbing the family. One day they joined a large deer-hunting party on the middle fork of the Holston, but they spent more of their time with the young ladies of Abingdon who were entertaining some of their school friends from Richmond. Riding parties, picnics, and especially dancing in the evening made the neighborhood very gay.

Frank's older sister Mary had married Eugene's older brother William. Another older brother, my father, and Frank remained good friends for more than fifty years. Frank's father and the Blackfords' father were also good friends and political allies. Young Robertson and William Blackford served together on Stuart's staff during the war.

Captain Robertson's oldest daughter married Willoughby Reade when he was engaged to teach at the Episcopal High School in Alexandria, Virginia, twenty-nine years after Appomattox. I was born that summer, and about nine months later Frank Robertson Reade followed me into this world. We were brought up like brothers. His grandfather would visit us several weeks every winter at the school, so I knew him better than any of my father's brothers.

Frank Reade spent the summers (except the eventful one of 1918 when he was in France) at The Meadows, the family's home for many years. After World War I he earned his Ph.D. at the University of Virginia. For ten years he taught at the Georgia School of Technology, and he did so well he was promoted to the presidency of the Georgia State Women's College where he served with distinction until he retired on account of his health in 1947.

Long before his health failed, Frank had told me that his ambition was to write a book about his grandfather, whom he idolized.

Frank Robertson had written two accounts of his Civil War experiences, one in about 1906 and the other in 1926. Reade wanted to present these memoirs with suitable background and some comment. He also wanted to tell about The Meadows, a farm bought by his grandfather's grandfather, Captain Francis Smith, in 1823.[1] He wanted to depict "its people, its animals and its anecdotes,...the books, the joys, the sorrows, the songs, the music and the flowers of past years," and the five generations of the family that had lived there. His dual responsibilities in running both the Women's College and Camp Glenrochie, the girl's camp started by his mother in 1901, left little time for other things.

After his death in 1957 Mrs. Reade allowed me to have the uncompleted manuscript with many of his notes, in the hope that I could get the book ready for publication. The notes are tantalizing; they contain bits of humor, poetry and pathos, but they are rather fragmentary for any one else to work from. Nobody could complete the book as he would have done; indeed nobody now living knows enough about The Meadows to finish the book he wanted to write.

This work then is based on the letters Captain Robertson wrote from 1859 to 1865 and a few he received, the two sets of memoirs he wrote many years later, and what his grandson started. Study of the *Official Records of the War of the Rebellion* and of several biographies has proven the essential accuracy of the memoirs. I have done my best to preserve their spirit. This is the last thing I can do for my friend.

Dr. L. Minor Blackford
Atlanta
October 1, 1960

Preface

Dr. L. Minor Blackford

At Chancellorsville General J. E. B. Stuart, already a famous cavalry leader though only thirty years old, won international fame. Constantly with him during that battle was a newly appointed member of his staff who had yet to win his spurs, Assistant Engineer Frank Smith Robertson, eight years his junior. A deep attachment between the two men was born of the trials during that fearful and glorious day. This book portrays that friendship, so far as possible in their own words. Though Stuart met the death he expected a year later, Robertson fought on to the end of the war.

Like many other Confederate veterans, in starting life anew after Appomattox, Robertson displayed a courage equal to that he had shown on the field of battle, courage of a different sort, perhaps of a rarer kind, but nevertheless true. And for more than sixty years after the guns had grown cold Captain Robertson cherished an affectionate letter from General Stuart expressing admiration of his behavior under fire.

Acknowledgements

Dr. L. Minor Blackford

Many persons have helped in the preparation of this book. Perhaps first should be listed members of the clan:

Frank Robertson Reade's sister, Evelyn (Mrs. Paul E. Johnson) has done a lot of editorial work. She and her sister, Mary Willoughby (Mrs. William B. Copenhaver) have also contributed many little items about life at The Meadows.

The Captain's surviving son-in-law, Dr. J. Coleman Motley, father of Captain Motley[2] and present owner of The Meadows, has entertained me there and showed me many relics, and he has checked the manuscript. His daughter Katy (Mrs. Homer Grandstaff) has helped too.

Mrs. W. Y. C. White, daughter-in-law of the Captain's sister, Kate, and her daughter, Madge (Mrs. G. Emory Baya) have advised me as to many details.

Frank Robertson Blackford, son of Pelham Blackford, grandson of Colonel William W. Blackford, has given me permission to quote from Colonel Blackford's comments on von Borcke's book. His brother James Baylor Blackford has supplied me with the unpublished memoirs of Miss Gay Robertson Blackford.

Major General Edward W. Smoth U.S.A.R. Ret., Colonel William Couper, of V. M. I., and Colonel Allen P. Julian, U.S.A. Ret., have checked various military details and helped with advice along other lines.

1

The University of Virginia

In the fall of the year the flaming colors of the maples and the dogwoods make the University of Virginia, with its classic pavilions and colonnades, even lovelier. To this place of simple beauty in 1859 were drawn more than five hundred young men in quest of higher learning. They came from all over the South, and even a few from beyond the Mason-Dixon Line. Among them were, of course, a few who hoped the South would secede from the Union and, if war ensued, so much the better. Others feared that, even without bloodshed, the South might break up the Union. Most of them, however, were amiable young gentlemen who wanted nothing more than to be allowed to continue with their friends the uninterrupted pursuit of their studies in this idyllic spot.

One of these was Frank Smith Robertson, a slender, good-looking fellow of eighteen, with straight black hair and high cheek bones suggesting the blood of Pocahontas which flowed in his veins. The old Virginia families felt that this strain, found in so many of them, made the blood even bluer (and they still do). Frank's father, Wyndham Robertson[1], was more proud of being a descendant of the Indian princess than of having been governor of Virginia.

During the summer of 1859 young Frank Robertson, when not riding or fishing, dancing or picnicking, had been busy getting ready to enroll at the university. He had not given much thought as yet to the crisis confronting the nation, or if he did it is not recorded, and was concerned only with acquiring an education. At the same time, however, about a hundred miles north of the university, across the Potomac River from the mouth of the Shenandoah River, a bearded stranger was busying himself mysteriously with his sons on a rented farm. Visitors were not welcomed there, for plans were being formulated that would interrupt Robertson's and his fellow students' quiet fall days and give the issue confronting the North and the South a new and terrible importance.

On Sunday night, October 16, 1859, the prevailing calm of Harpers Ferry was rudely shattered by a madman's bloody invasion. That night the bearded stranger with eighteen armed followers crossed the Potomac, picked up hostages along the way, and seized the United States Arsenal. His avowed intent was to incite the slaves to revolt, but when this did not happen he and his followers herded nine of their most prominent hostages into a windowless brick fire engine house. Neither the mob nor the local militia saw fit to storm this citadel.

When news of the insurrection reached Washington on Monday morning, Lieutenant J. E. B. Stuart, on leave from his post in Kansas, happened to be in the War Department. He was sent across the river to Arlington to summon Lieutenant Colonel Robert E. Lee.

That afternoon Colonel Lee, Lieutenant Stuart, who had volunteered as his aide, and Lieutenant Israel Green, with ninety Marines under his command, were sent by the president to restore order at Harpers Ferry.

Early the next day Stuart approached the engine house "in the presence of perhaps two thousand spectators" to demand surrender. He "recognized old Osawatomie Brown who had given us so much trouble in Kansas."[2] When John Brown refused to surrender, Stuart waved his hat and the Marines battered down the heavy doors. Brown was turned over to the civil authorities and a few days later placed

Governor Wyndham Robertson, father of Frank S. Robertson.

on trial in Charles Town, charged with "treason, and conspiring with slaves and other rebels, and of murder in the first degree." After a fair trial—and it has never been denied that he received a fair trial,—he was sentenced to hang on December 2, 1859. It would be impossible to exaggerate the impact of this raid on the country, both North and South. The idea of a white man trying to lead slaves in a revolt and the inevitable bloodshed that must follow was unspeakably horrible to Virginians.

In New England, on the other hand, the Abolitionists promptly apotheosized Brown and gave Virginia reason to believe that another and larger invasion of the state was being planned to rescue him. That the Northerners could even condone Brown's plan was hard on Southern sensibilities; that they could contemplate insulting the dignity of Virginia by an attempt to save him inflamed passion. Governor Henry A. Wise determined to forestall any such attempt.[3] To preserve order he called out not only the militia, but also the state's pride, the cadets of the Virginia Military Institute. He had more than 1,500 soldiers present at the execution. The impact of these events was not lost on the students of the university. Robertson was among those who took a special interest in the affair and two days before the hanging he wrote from the university to his father in Richmond:

> There has been a great deal of excitement here, since the Cadets passed through, and the military spirit is so universal that I believe there are very few, who would not prefer, at present, changing the pen for the musket. There has been a Volunteer company formed: there were about 200 names put down for enlistment, but a great many were later taken off. They offered their services to the Governor in case aid was required at Charles Town, and yesterday received a dispatch requesting them to hold themselves in readiness to march at a moment's warning. The prevailing opinion is, however, that they would be the last body of men in the state that would be called on.
>
> I am very glad to see that you were appointed Captain of the Home Guard, and also that the company had not followed the advice of the Dispatch and chosen as their uniform, hunting shirts of gray home spun goods, especially as it is composed principally of the oldest and most respectable citizens, I hear.

The gap between North and South only deepened in the months that followed. War talk increased, and other groups of men and boys formed militia companies and ordered fancy uniforms. Meanwhile the nation prepared for the coming election which would decide the issue for many people on both sides of the Mason-Dixon Line. After the votes were cast the time of choosing sides began. Frank wrote to his father five days after the November 1860 election:

I suppose you are all participators in the excitement which pervades the South concerning the result of the election. It has been intense here and nothing is talked about, but the all-absorbing topic, secession. Every day a large crowd assembles around the Post Office and anxiously awaiting the opening that they may learn the news, and the prevailing impression is, I think, that the University will suspend before Christmas. As to myself, I have no definite opinion of what will be the result of the present state of affairs. I can only judge from what I see in the papers, and they have a tendency to exaggerate. I think the same may be said of the students: even on the day of election, it was reported, and believed by some, that South Carolina had seceded, and ever since, reports and rumors of different kinds have been in circulation through College until it is impossible to obtain a clue as to the true condition of things. I would be glad if you would write me your views on the subject soon, as I am quite anxious to hear them. The majority of the students, I think, are secessionists, and I noticed yesterday that quite a number had mounted the cockade.[4] I understood two hundred were sold yesterday at the Bookstore.

The governor had taken his daughter, Kate, on a little trip for health and recreation, spending two or three days in Washington and then going on to Baltimore. He was not able to answer his son until November 17, 1860:

I wish to make a suggestion or two on the subject that excites your very natural solicitude. A young man can never err, in the absence of an active emergency, in refusing to take extreme courses. Now it is not a question of what to do, but of what to think. May not a young man naturally distrust his ability to come to certain conclusions on questions so great and so difficult as those now agitating the country? To feel and express a just resentment at the hostile tone— and the disloyal conduct of so many of the Northern people,—and to be indignant and aggrieved at being defeated by a mere sectional vote,—such things are not inconsistent with a refusal to decide, in advance of this State and of one's elders, what course is best to be pursued, and, of course, to refuse to join in measures that imply that the course of the State is settled.

A just indulgence and expression of opinions and resentments, natural under the offensive course and attitude of the North I see no occasion to with-hold,—but to decide what should be done appears to me to be more modest and more becoming for young men not to determine before their States...have adopted their course. Then, if wholly inconsistent with your ideas, and intolerable to your sense of what the case demanded after due reflection and due consideration, I would concur that a young man of your age [Frank was not yet 20], if clear and sure in his own judgment, should not yield his convictions entirely to anybody.

I think, however, a just distrust under such grave circumstances as exist would recommend a refusal to take any active or positive measures in advance of one's State.

While his election to high office eleven years before Frank was born suggests that Wyndham Robertson was not without powers of persuasion and other political gifts, this letter indicates also a deep respect for his son's individuality.[5]

It cannot be concluded from these thoughtful letters Frank wrote from the university that all his time was devoted to consideration of the grave national issues of the day. He had his share of fun. Among other extra-curricular activities, he joined Eugene Blackford's cricket club.[6] Each member of that choice little organization would soon be a Confederate soldier; perhaps the one who achieved the widest renown was Sandy Pendleton.[7] Frank wrote in his memoirs:

> I was a student at the University of Virginia in 1860-'61. War talk was rife and studying slack. For several months before Virginia seceded, excitement was tense among the students, and in no similar institution in the United States was the great question of secession so exhaustively and strenuously discussed,—from the faculty down to the merest kid.... The students, some 500, were divided in their views, though the majority opposed secession, that is, until every reasonable effort had been made to avert it. I thought, as did my father, that the secession of Virginia should come only as a last resort. I felt that whatever Virginia did it was my duty to approve.
>
> One night in December, 1860, I went over to Dawson's Row to call on two of my intimates, William [B.] Tabb[8] of Amelia and [W.] Page McCarty[9] of Richmond. We spread out on the beds after the student style of the day, and the conversation ran at once to war talk. Tabb was a graduate of the Virginia Military Institute, and I remember perfectly saying to him, "Tabb, why don't you get up a company of students, and we'll all go to war together?" This remark opened up the subject and resulted in the organization of the two companies of students who assisted in the capture of Harpers Ferry [four months] later.
>
> We three organized that night, and applied to the faculty the next day to permit a military organization at the very staid and peaceful old University. It was accorded at once,[10] to our surprise, and our company was fully ranked immediately; a second company was organized a day or two later.

These companies were commanded respectively by William Tabb and Ned Hutter[11] of Lynchburg, and the awkward squads were soon in full possession of the Lawn. My military education being limited, I was simply noted for being one of the originators of this military move, being made first corporal. The officers as a rule were graduates of V. M. I.

Uniforms were ordered from Baltimore, consisting of red flannel shirts, black pants, dark blue caps, white cross belts with brass buckles. My company was named by Professor [James P.] Holcombe,[12] "The Sons of Liberty." The other company, "The Southern Guard," was similarly uniformed, except that the shirts were blue and the caps light blue.

South Carolina seceded on December 20, 1860. In January, Mississippi, Florida, Alabama, Georgia, and Louisiana followed her out of the Union. No wonder the young men at the University of Virginia were in turmoil. Wyndham Robertson refused to admit that the grand old state which had done so much to form the Union, must eventually and inevitably secede too. He continued to correspond with Northern leaders,[13] such as General Winfield Scott,[14] a Virginian by birth, Washington Hunt, who had been governor of New York, and Samuel J. Tilden, who was also to serve as governor of New York, though not as president of the United States.

An example of this correspondence is found in a letter from General Scott to Governor Robertson, dated February 19, 1861:

> I have had no letter nor oral assurance from Mr. Lincoln, or from any one likely to come into his Cabinet, on the subject, but I think I can say with confidence that the idea of coercing any seceded state by an army in the field will be eschewed by the incoming administration. Should I discover myself to be in error in that impression, I shall hasten to tell you so.
>
> I have a lively hope,—a reasonable expectation—that the new Cabinet, in less than three months—probably in less than a month—will openly support a plan of conciliation or compromise...as liberal as Crittenden's Resolution.

Though the General stipulated that his letter should not be given to the press, he requested that it be shown "to my friends, [Alexander H. H.] Stuart,[15] [Williams C.] Wickham,[16] of the [Virginia] Senate.... Show it also to friends, [James Edward] MacFarland,[17] and Alex Rives."[18]

How tragically mistaken the old military was! Robertson's memoir continues:

That spring Pa wrote to me to come to Richmond and attend the great Convention being held there to determine Virginia's course. This I did, and I returned to the University much less a secessionist than ever, and I had several disagreeable discussions with some of my friends of opposite views.

When news that Fort Sumter had been fired on reached the students, "a tremendous shout was raised on the Lawn, and the cry, 'fight, fight, fight.'"[19] In his memoirs Robertson said not a word about the feelings of the young men at the University on receipt of this intelligence, but he did preserve a letter from his father who wrote from Richmond on April 13, 1861:

Yesterday was a day of tremendous excitement here. The knowledge that actual war—bombardments and strife were in actual progress between our own brethren—could not but intensely excite the public passion. The Convention, without acting on the question, was yet a scene of some very excited debate. In the evening the whole town was all ablaze with tar barrels and torches,—shaken for hours with the firing off of cannon,—and of speeches. I did not, as you may suppose, attend or take part in the hullyballoo. I see nothing in Civil War to rejoice over, be who may the victor. Yet I consider Lincoln's course utterly infamous as well as wholly unwarranted by Law, and wish all confusion and defeat to his counsels and plans. His silence and stillness has been like the tiger's preparatory to his leap. I feared and called attention to it in the Whig of last Saturday, and urged sending a commission to Washington to demand to know his purpose. The same evening resolutions to that effect were offered in the Convention, and Commissioners sent,[20]—but they were already too late— orders and troops, now engaged along our Southern Coast were already on their way—the whole country being kept ignorant of the scheme. What an idea of Government—to steal on its people like a thief in the night....

I suppose you all partake so much of the prevailing excitement as to do little in the way of study. Tell me how it is—and whether, as the saying goes, you are doing any good? Here there is such a state of things that I don't believe you would now derive much benefit or knowledge from being here. In the Convention there is less of calm or useful discussion now, than mere quarreling—and snarling—while out of doors there is little to hear or see worth hearing or seeing.

The bombardment had begun on April 12. Fort Sumter surrendered on the 14th. The next day Lincoln called for 75,000 volunteers.

2

The First Two Years

With the fall of Fort Sumter Robertson and the rest of the university's "soldiers" were greatly excited about what would happen next. In his memoirs he recorded:

On April 16 the day before Virginia seceded a rumor spread like wildfire that our Battalion was ordered "somewhere". No one knew where. My Unionism evaporated rapidly, and I was going to go, — nolens volens[1], — but, remembering that my father had told me always to ask permission when going away from the University, in full regalia I rushed to see Dr. [Socrates] Maupin [Chairman of the Faculty], and walked in on a full meeting of the Faculty. I attempted to withdraw, but was ordered to stay.

"Can I go with my Company?"

"Where?"

"Don't know, sir."

"Are you 21?"

"No, sir."

"Sorry, but I can't give you my permission."

"A smile pervaded that august body, — indeed it was on when I entered. It was followed by an almost outburst when I said,

"Sorry, Doctor, but I'll have to go anyway."

The mysterious was abroad. No one knew anything except that we were ordered somewhere. The companies were called and, as for various reasons some of the boys could not go, sundry changes occurred in the personnel of our Company. Our Captain was too sick and our 1st Lieutenant James [T.] Tosh[2] became Captain. In the changes I became orderly sergeant, the most onerous and disagreeable position in the ranks. I at once made out the new roll, and calling, "Fall in, fall in," lined up the Company, and at the command, "Right face, forward march," off we marched in column of fours to Charlottesville. After a wait of several hours, a freight train rolled up about 10 PM, and we were loaded into filthy cattle cars, and off we started for the mysterious somewhere.

The State had furnished us with flintlock muskets but no flints, cartridge boxes but no cartridges; we carried no overcoats, no blankets, no haversacks, no tin cups, — nothing indeed but ourselves.... We made no claims to being immaculate when we unloaded at Strasburg at daylight the next morning.

Our first skirmish was for breakfast. Our first march was 18 miles over rough macadam road to Winchester. Tight boots and tough language cheered us on the way. We reached Winchester some time after dark, and marched down the street behind a local band playing Yankee Doodle and amid numerous cheers for the Union. Divided into squads of ten, we partook of the hospitality of the Secesh citizens and swept their tables clean, having had nothing to eat worth mentioning since we left the University. About midnight, flints, but no cartridges, were distributed to the boys. Again boarding a freight train, we were soon bouncing along towards Harpers Ferry, which place we reached at dawn."

The Federals marched out without a shot being fired. For certain aforesaid causes, our firing would have been perforce equally silent. The great arsenals were burning, and we could see thousands of red hot muskets going out of commission. Virginia's glorious flag was run up the tall U. S. flagpole, and we veterans went into camp in the depot. Search parties soon found plenty of arms, generally hidden by the citizens between their mattresses. Whether this was done for the good of the North or for the good of the South, I do not know. As the people of Harpers Ferry were almost a unit for the Union, we must suppose the former, though it miscarried in favor of the latter most beautifully, as many hundreds of good, up-to-date arms were thus secured. Our companies were at once put on a sure-enough war footing with the best arms of the day and plenty of ammunition.

Four days we played soldier at Harpers Ferry, and strenuous days they were to such greenhorns. Then the Governor in a most complimentary order commending our work and patriotism, ordered our return to the University and disbanding, saying, among other things, that there was too much talent to be risked in one body. Our return to our Alma Mater differed greatly from our departure. Even this bloodless taste of war opened up a vista of what was to come not before realized. We disbanded a sadder, if not a wiser, lot of boys. The date of our disbanding I don't recall, but it must have been about April 23.[3]

On April 27 Frank received a letter from his father.

> If you could, you ought to have informed us, at such a time, where
> you were, and what doing. Since you got back [from Harpers Ferry],
> we still have only messages, which I do not fully understand....
> You want to know if I still desire you to quit college and come
> here. I do not at present see any adequate object. I learn your com-
> pany is a fine one and that you like it.... I do not know that you could
> be more usefully employed, in a military view, than where you are,
> and where doubtless, perfecting yourselves in the military art is now
> a prominent part of your engagements (and ought to be). At least for
> the present. There must be a brief pause now, I think, before it can
> be fully determined whether we are to have a regular and protracted
> war—or peace. The former is most probable—by far—but not quite
> certain. Till this question is solved, I think you could hardly be bet-
> ter employed anywhere, than where you are.... But let me hear from
> you and hear your views. Do you like, as I hear you do, your Com-
> pany? And officers? What office have you?
> I am not sure you decided best in declining the lieutenancy some
> time ago, though the reason was highly commendable. In service,
> however, rank tells very sensibly. Is there any prospect of promotion
> soon? Your Capt., [William E.] Jones,[4] is here on the tent business,—
> leaving Mr. [William W.] Blackford[5] to do the military (in Camp, I
> believe) in Abingdon. The Company is not [yet] ordered into service.
> I think of sending for some of the horses, say the grays and Comet,
> perhaps a fourth. One I should like to give Tom Semmes, who is
> Adjutant, I think. What say you to his having Comet? He was never
> a favorite of yours.[6]
> The Home Guard is now a Battalion of 500 oldsters, of which I
> am Lieut. Col.

Proud of his son's conduct at Harpers Ferry, Governor Robertson
wrote Frank again on the 30th. He enclosed the check for a hundred dollars that had been asked for, and authorized him to "close
up everything at the University, and come here." He also promised to "make all due inquiry as to the proper arrangement at Lexington—and look around to see what may be best for you."
Robertson continued in his memoirs:

> Having become a veteran, and war having been declared, of course,
> the resumption of my civil education was not to be considered. Ac-
> cordingly, I bade a sad farewell to the old University and my many
> dear friends, and went home to Richmond, where I at once joined the
> Richmond Howitzers as a private. My father, however, said the Con-
> federacy needed officers who knew something of drill, and my name
> was stricken from the rolls.[7]

Lt. Col. William Willis Blackford, engineer officer to Maj. Gen. J. E. B. Stuart from June 24, 1862 to February 19, 1864. He was a captain while on the staff but rose to the rank of lieutenant colonel in the First Regiment of Engineers. Blackford married Frank Robertson's sister, Mary.

A few days later an official document came to me, a commission as 2nd lieutenant in the Provisional or Regular Army of Virginia, with orders to report at once to the Commandant of the Virginia Military Institute to be drilled. Infantry, cavalry and artillery tactics were driven into us by main force. Two months this went on without a break, and in the meantime war and rumors of war were rife in the land.

Frank wrote to his father from V.M.I. on June 30, 1861:

Your long expected letter arrived this morning and it afforded me relief,—not that it contained very encouraging news concerning my office, but from the fact that so many contradictory rumors were afloat about the disbanding of the Provisional, that authentic news of any sort offered relief even when adverse to one's wishes. I have been laid up for the last two days with a strained ankle caused by placing my foot on a piece of leather while going through the Zouave drill—it is so much better this morning that I think I shall go to church.

I think it probable business will be suspended here in a day or two—there have been no lectures in tactics for upwards of a week, and great numbers of the cadets have left in disgust, many more intend leaving tomorrow and the next day—three of the Instructors leave also tomorrow, which will leave only one that is a capable drill master. I am sure there is very bad mismanagement somewhere, but who is to blame I don't know. I will write again in a day or two and let you know what turn affairs take.

You wish to know what to do with my uniform, etc. The rifle I would prefer keeping, but the uniform I think I shall scarcely need; the sword is totally unfit for service, though I expect it will be difficult to get another.

The weather lately has been exceedingly warm, and as we have been drilling in the Bayonet exercise and required to stand in one place, I felt it severely, but on that account I appreciate the more highly my nightly bath in the river. There is a beautiful place about 400 yards from the Institute and a party of us go down every night.

Not long after he wrote this letter Robertson was gone from the Institute. He wrote years later that he was, "Afraid that the War would end without my assistance, one evening in pure desperation I took the night stage for Salem,[8] and reached Abingdon in the morning." He need not have worried.

The Governor was kept busy in Richmond. He was in correspondence with his kinsman, Colonel John Arthur Campbell,[9] a V.M.I. graduate, class of 1844, at that time organizing in Abingdon the 48th Virginia Infantry, about a commission for his son in that regiment. He was also careful to see that the boy was not listed as a deserter from the Institute, for in his files was found this note:

Head Quarters, Richmond
July 3rd, '61

Wyndham Robertson, Esq.,
Richmond

Sir,

In pursuance of our conversation this morning, I take pleasure in enclosing a copy of the order relieving your son from duty in Lexington, which I hope will prove satisfactory to you. I have enclosed a copy also to Col. Smith, Superintendent V.M.I. who will see that he is properly informed in the matter.

Very Resp'ly
Your obedient servant
R. E. Lee

Robertson's next assignment was duly recorded in his memoirs:

The 48th Virginia Infantry was in process of formation, and I joined it. It was made up of big mountaineers from Southwest Virginia. These "mountain boomers" were highly independent, and had no use for discipline. Will [Y. C.] Hannum,[10] a V.M.I. boy and 1st lieutenant, and myself had to drill this mob daily, a company at a time. My drill included 500 men and officers. It was a job. I would say, "Hold your head up. Put your feet together. Put your hands

down. Look like a soldier." Response: "You go to hell." They were
fine soldiers in battle, but difficult in barracks. But a week after I
joined, Company I (Captain James Campbell[11] commanding) elected
me 1st lieutenant.

Soon we were ordered to western Virginia. Nine days march from
Staunton we camped on Valley Mountain,—and many, many poor boys
are camped there still. It rained for forty days and nights. Our rations were fresh beef and flour: only this and nothing more. We had
no salt for our beef, no grease for our bread and only a frying pan to
cook in. The results were immediate and fatal to a degree. Cornmeal
and bacon will do even without cooking utensils,—but fresh beef and
flour—no salt and no ovens—will be as death-dealing as the plague.
We had a surgeon, but no medicine. Hundreds were sick and many
died. Forty men in my company of eighty-seven had measles. There
is no disease worse under exposure. It was terrible to hear through
the night the cries of those dying boys calling for mothers, wives and
sisters. Ninety per cent of them had never been away from home
before. There were fourteen in my company at roll call when I made
my last appearance.

I broke down with camp fever, which made me unconscious of all
things.[12] A retreat was ordered and a detail of my company carried
me on a litter for four days. It seems like a dream now,—it seemed
like a dream then. My father met me with a little carriage at the
Greenbrier River and took me back to The Meadows.

Robertson probably returned home in October 1861 and after a
period of recuperation rejoined his regiment. He wrote to his father from Winchester on January 17, 1862:

I reached this place Monday night after a safe but most disagreeable trip. I had the misfortune to fall in with a drunken crowd, (as
indeed one seldom fails to do now) & was entertained by its delightful proceedings all the way to Manassas, where much to my satisfaction it was disposed of by the Police.

On reaching Strasburg we had to take an Omnibus with no fire
in it, to Winchester & I became so chilled in spite of my overcoat, that
immediately on my arrival I was attacked with Cholic [colic], accompanied by Rheumatism pretty severely in both arms I immediately
went to bed, & tho' my attack of Cholic [colic] was not so bad as the
last I had, I am still "hors de combat," not however so much from its
effects, as from Rheumatism in my arms. I am afraid it is a more
serious affair than I at first supposed & am at present rather at a
loss what to do as I am sure my condition is not such as to admit of
my joining my Reg', indeed Dr. Conrad whom I advised on the subject
today, says I am totally unfit for service & recommends my return
home at once.

I hope however, and it is generally believed, that Gen. [Thomas J.] Jackson will go into Winter Quarters soon & I could then go into camp without running much risk. I shall at any rate remain in my present quarters a while, until something definite is known concerning his future movements. His officers condemn his present course as being the most unwise he could pursue. He is marching his men about all over the country thro' snow & ice, for the accomplishment of things for which it is generally thought he is by no means repaid by the immense number it makes sick, & by the general discontent it gives rise to among the men. I have heard twenty say, that if he persisted much longer in his present course, there would scarcely be a man in his army that would re-enlist. Numbers are __ [mounting] in sick every day & it is reported that there are three thousand at present sick in Winchester. He is now I hear 15 miles beyond Romney & where he is bound no one can guess as it is proverbial that he never lets anyone know what his intentions are.

I am presently boarding at a private house (Mrs. Hopkins, some kin I believe to Cousin Anna) & am very comfortably quartered. I am rooming with two Lieutenants in Jackson's Brigade, who are also on the sick list, & who I find very agreeable companions.

Cousin Mary is staying here also, but speaks of going on to Romney if the Reg' is to stay in that neighborhood any time.

In a skirmish a few days since the 48th behaved beautifully I hear & was very much complimented by the Gen' [Jackson]. One of my men was shot thro' the leg & another had the stock of his musket shot away. One of Milt White's men was also wounded.[13] A good many officers from [Col. Samuel V.] Fulkerson's Reg' are here sick, but I have seen __ [word illegible] from the 48th.[14] Please let me hear from you soon. Direct to the care of Mrs. Hopkins, Winchester.

Robertson's condition had improved little when he again wrote to his father on January 19:

When I left you I supposed there would be little difficulty in getting a furlough in case my attack of Rheumatism increased, especially by showing the note Dr. Gibson gave me. I learn from Dr. Carrington that it is Jackson's express orders that no furloughs should be granted, no matter what the circumstances,—he also states that he is prohibited from giving men even a certificate of unfitness for duty, which I supposed by sending on, might be the means of getting a furlough. My only chance of getting on therefore is to go on to my Regt and apply personally, which is however an expedition I am decidedly opposed to taking in my present condition, as it is more than probable that I could not get one, besides running the risk of being thrown back by exposure.

Dr. Conrad whom I have consulted about it, seems to think that my surest chance would be to send you a certificate of my condition and get you to apply to the Sec. of War for a furlough. He says that the Rheumatism in my arms has a tendency to affect my heart and that a return to service for some time would certainly bring about serious results. He considers it at present a matter of no great importance, but urges my immediate return home, where I may better be subjected to medical treatment. Enclosed therefore I send you the medical certificate, hoping you may be enabled to get me a furlough in the manner described. If you do not succeed, I will probably have to resign, which I should dislike very much, as I should no doubt be fit for duty again in a month or two.

I am in first rate quarters and tomorrow will get another room, where Jimmy White and myself will be to ourselves. I wrote to you that our forces are 15 miles beyond Romney,—it is a mistake,—three of our regiments are several miles only beyond. The enemy are reported as fortifying on the R.R. about 16 miles beyond Romney, but as so many rumors are afloat it is hard to get at the truth.

Robertson's health remained fragile. He recounted in his memoirs what happened:

This illness was so severe and its effects so lasting that, though I reported for duty several times, it finally resulted in my being "sent home to die," as the M.D. told me. The Board of Examiners in Richmond credited me with pericarditis. They discharged me from the army and advised a sea voyage. While considering this, I had a letter from Colonel Campbell, offering me the adjutantcy of my old regiment. During my absence from the regiment, there had been the general reorganization of the army, and the rank and file were allowed to elect their officers. Many of the old officers lost their positions; myself among them owing to my company having heard of my discharge from the army. I determined to throw up the European trip and accept the adjutantcy, and immediately went to report to Colonel Campbell. Ere I could reach him at Harrisonburg, he had been put in command of the Brigade [a post he did not hold long for he was wounded near Winchester June 2, 1862, but the Brigade retained his name for more than a year after that], and the lieutenant colonel thus became commander of the 48th. He had appointed Lieutenant Hale as his adjutant. My old company held a meeting at once and elected me their captain, their newly elected officers agreeing to drop back one place to admit of this. This was a great compliment certainly, but I was unwilling to accept, not only that I disliked to have these officers make the sacrifice, but I was convinced that I was in no condition to become again a foot soldier.

On my return to Richmond, my father set to work securing me a
passport from Mr.[George Wythe] Randolph,[15] Secretary of War, letters to friends in Europe, cash and clothes. All was ready for me to
sail on a blockade runner from Savannah, when General J. E. B. Stuart
called at our house to see Captain William W. Blackford, who was on
his staff. Hearing that I was sick, he honored me with a call also,
and came to my room. He found me in bed, reading a medical work;
he promptly advised me for my own betterment to "throw it in the
fire." He asked me a few questions about the campaign in western
Virginia. It was my first view of him.

Frank Robertson never wrote out a description of his hero, but
many other men did. General Stuart was a big man, broad-shoul-
dered and powerful. His pale blue eyes could flash fire or sparkle
with merriment. His ruddy complexion was well tanned; his nos-
trils were large and mobile. A heavy reddish-brown mustache and
beard with highlights of bronze covered the lower part of his face
and neck. Calling at the home of a distinguished civilian, he was
wearing a well tailored uniform of grey broadcloth with gleaming
galloons on the sleeves. Shiny brass buttons in pairs and a yellow
sash heavily betasseled completed his finery for the golden spurs
had not yet been given him. His light grey felt hat, pinned up on
the right, with the black ostrich plume, and the generously cut grey
cloak, lined by Mrs. Stuart with scarlet silk, did not go into the
sick room, but he was wearing
his high, well polished cavalry
boots.

*Maj. Gen. James Ewell Brown
Stuart, chief of cavalry of the
Army of Northern Virginia.*

The renowned cavalry leader, overflowing with health and strength, saw in the bed before him more than a wasted young invalid. Frank noted the results of the meeting:

> A week or so later a note came from him offering me a position on his staff. I didn't want to go to Europe, and felt that, in the nature of things, I wouldn't be satisfied to be away from Virginia in her hour of stress. So, knowing I would have a horse instead of my weak legs to tote me, and thinking perhaps this might enable me to stand the service, I accepted the proffered post.

But it would be many long months before Robertson's fragile health would allow him to assume these duties. A few days after General Stuart's call, Governor Robertson took his son back to the mountains. On June 7, a week after the Confederates had halted the Federal army at the gates of their capital, and a week after General Robert E. Lee had taken command of the Army of Northern Virginia, Frank wrote from The Meadows to his father who had returned to Richmond. Though unable to take the field with the army Frank kept busy at home breaking horses:

> Your letter reached us yesterday & confirmed my fear of your detention. We also received three or four Richmond papers, bringing the first news from that point for several days—the wires were down & it was impossible to even hear why the train was detained.
>
> I suppose ere this you are safe in Richmond & really I begin to feel very much like being there too. I find it impossible to become reconciled to leading this quiet, inactive life at home, even when convinced that it is for the best. I have however improved very much since my arrival here and with the exception of occasional pain in my heart and arm, feel almost as strong as ever. A week longer I hope will enable me to take the field—in what capacity I find it hard to determine. Infantry is the arm of the service I prefer, but without an office not suited either to my health or inclination. Cavalry I would rather enter as a private than anything else, but I know no company in which I am well enough acquainted to make it agreeable,—while the place offered me by Gen. Stuart is one I would rather not accept, if my health admits of service elsewhere. Please find out the usual outfit of a Volunteer Aid and let me know. I think it probable an aid to General Stuart would require two horses.
>
> I am glad you have determined to have the young horses broken—with the assistance of Sam, I shall go to work tomorrow.[16]
>
> Monday June 8th
>
> I should have finished this letter & sent it yesterday, but Ma who was also writing to you, advised me to __ [word illegible] a day which

I fear will amount to two as I have been so occupied all day with the horses as to neglect it until after supper, & I believe the mail closes at eight.

So far I have succeeded admirably. I first put the __ [word illegible] filly & Rieves little sorrel in the buggy, & after three or four hours drive, brought them back working beautifully. I next put one of the match bays & one of the work horses in Davidson's light two horse wagon & gave her a two hours trot up & down the bottom in the field next to Bett's—having been worked before several times in the off lead, she soon became accustomed to the pole & double lines. I then took her out & put in her place the little bay horse Mr. Lipford has been riding. He had never been in harness before but with the exception of being awkward, gave very little trouble showing no disposition to either kick or run. I drove him the rest of the evening & thus finished the day. Tomorrow I shall devote to the more thorough breaking of those I have commenced with. Do you wish Wyndham's horse broken & the sorrel Mr. Lipford rides—the latter will make an excellent riding horse & it is almost a pity to work her.

Robertson spent the rest of the month at the Meadows, but as his health improved he decided to go to the family's home in Richmond. He arrived on the evening of July 4 to find the city engulfed with the wounded from the Seven Days fighting and in the midst of a stifling heat wave. He wrote to his father the next day:

We reached here safely last night about nine o'clock, being detained at the junction four or five hours by the non arrival of the up train, which was unable to pass the wreck of the day before....

It is almost impossible to hear anything reliable from the Army. As far as I can judge, however, things are pretty much at a stand still at present & much apprehension is felt that the Federals will cross the River & escape. It is rumored this evening that two of their Divisions are so placed that their capture is certain. I hope so indeed, for the capture of their whole army would hardly more than repay for the immense loss we have suffered. The whole city is in mourning & scarcely a lady is seen not in black....

I saw Dr. Minor today. He says he heard from Mr. [William W.] Blackford a few days since & he was safe. Gilbert was here yesterday before I arrived, he expected to join Mr. B today & return tomorrow.[17]

Cousin William thinks he can probably let me have Cousin James horse, but if Gilbert returns tomorrow I can possibly get one of Mr. Blackfords. I think you had better keep an eye to the Grey we were looking at. If sound he is fully worth 250.

Robertson wrote again on the seventh, but this time to his mother:

> I am still unable to hear of the whereabouts of Mr. Blackford. Gilbert was in the habit of coming in every day in two, until I came, but has not been heard of since. The horse Cousin William thought of lending me, was taken off by __ [words illegible], & the one left in his place is lame, so that I shall probably still be in town a day or two unless I disappear in a grease spot, which I think imminent if this warm weather continues much longer....
>
> Indeed if this weather continues, I don't know what will become of the sick & wounded. I understand 80 died at the Winder Hospital day before yesterday, 83 yesterday & if they die in proportion to the heat, it must have reached 100 today....
>
> I have seen several who came up from the Army yesterday. Nothing of importance going on & little prospect of a fight soon. The Federals are heavily reinforcing....
>
> Numbers of people are passing into town by every train—some to look after wounded relations, while others under the belief that Richmond is no longer in danger are returning to their homes. I hope it may be so, but many believe the worst is yet to come.

Though Richmond slowly began to recover Robertson did not. Despite his eagerness to secure a horse and ride out of the city his health would not permit it. He expressed his frustration in a letter to his father on July 20:

> Much against my will I am still here—too much of an invalid to join the General.
>
> I still suffer considerably with pain in my head and shoulders and the Dr. says I must remain perfectly quiet indoors until free from it—he now thinks it is produced, as I have all the time persisted, by a slight sunstroke and thinks to venture in the sun until free from pain, would be dangerous. I am engaged therefore at present in obeying his injunctions most implicity & with the best grace possible under the circumstances. This is my third attempt in the last few months to re-enter the service and I confess I am discouraged at the results. I am slowly improving however and hope a few more days will restore me.
>
> I suppose ere this you have started Sam & the horses. I hope you did not send the ___ [word illegible] mare for her size will prevent her selling well & it is doubtful I will be allowed but one horse. Why would not the grey suit—& either Billy Bowlegs or the Sorrel.

All of Robertson's concern about horses would come to naught. He would not be joining Stuart in "a few more days."

At the time these letters were written Maj. Gen. George B. McClellan, having been driven back from the outskirts of the Confederate capital, was still sulking at Harrison's Landing on the James. The Confederates were satisfied that he had done his worst. Maj. Gen. John Pope was invading northern Virginia with another Federal army and vainglorious manifestos.[18] Stonewall Jackson had already set out after him. Stuart had just held one of his numerous cavalry reviews ten miles north of Richmond near Hanover Court House, and Wade Hampton[19] and Fitz Lee[20] were brand new brigadier generals of cavalry. It was hard on Frank Robertson to see the army move off without him, but if he had known that Second Manassas was in the offing, he would have been broken-hearted.

The remaining months of 1862 afford no additional letters from either Robertson, probably because father and son were together in Richmond. Robertson seemed no closer to joining Stuart than he had been at the end of 1861. However, his brother-in-law, Captain W. W. Blackford, already with Stuart as his engineer officer, was doing his best to see that Stuart would not forget the sickly young man he had visited in Richmond over a year earlier. Blackford wrote of his efforts to Wyndham Robertson on January 10, 1863:

> I have written to Mary to come on and pay me a visit, hoping the change of scene may benefit her at this time and direct her thoughts from our poor little Landon.[21] I wrote to ask Frank to accompany her as he would find much to interest him and would I think advance his interests by so doing.
>
> I have watched closely every opportunity to bring the mention of his joining us before the General and have had several conversations upon the subject with him. He has great reluctance to having an officer on his staff who draws no pay, and has several times asked me if you could not get Frank a commission so he would not be liable to this difficulty. I think if Frank could come on with his sister I might arrange it all—but at the same time I would not like to raise hopes in him, prematurely, for the staff is pretty full and I know that the General rejects a great many applicants constantly.

It is unknown whether Robertson accompanied his sister Mary on her visit to her husband's camp, though it is doubtful because of his condition. Nevertheless, Blackford's campaign met with some measure of success as a letter from Stuart to Wyndham Robertson indicates:

Hd. Qrs. Cav. Div.
January 14th, 1863

My much esteemed Friend,

I have been postponing [answering] your letter, as well as the very modest one written by your son previously, hoping that something would turn up to enable me to accept of his services as vol. aid. but this difficulty which I have been unable to remove is the avowed determination on my part to take no vol. aids [sic] other than those who have already served with me—this avowal (entre nous)[22] was made in consequence of efforts of objectionable persons to get such positions and by my being unable to get rid of their applications. This difficulty can be removed by your son's getting a commission and as officers of his experience and intelligence are needed in the Engineer and other corps, I think you ought to experience no difficulty in obtaining one and having him assigned to the Cavalry Division.

I will thus secure his services without embarrassment as I very much desire. Capt. Blackford has made me an elaborate sketch of the battlefield here which is to accompany Gen. R. E. Lee's report. It is considered excellent. I would like very much to have a visit from you to talk over various matters of interest. Won't you come?

Believe me
sincerely your friend
J. E. B. Stuart

P. S. Please communicate this to Frank.

Evidently as a result of his father's bestirring himself as suggested by General Stuart, Robertson was informed by J. F. Gilmer,[23] "Col. Engrs. and Chief of Eng. Bureau," on February 27, 1863, that he had been "appointed an Assistant Engineer," and was ordered to "report for duty to Maj. Gen. J. E. B. Stuart, Commanding Cavalry of the Army of Northern Virginia." His salary would be "Ninety (90) dollars per month."

Snow covered the ground the next day when Frank reported to General Stuart at Camp No-Camp, near Fredericksburg, the scene of the great Confederate victory the preceding December. On March 3 he found time to write to his father:

I am once more safely ensconced in a tent as a member of the Army, and the consciousness of being once more on duty in the field brings with it a pleasure even greater than I had anticipated and for the first time in 16 months I feel comparatively happy. The position I have is not such as I should choose or prefer, but I can already see and understand its duties sufficiently to consider myself competent with steady application and practice, to fulfill them. My only fear is that my health will give way, though I shall spare no precautions to prevent it.

I find Mr. B. [W. W. Blackford] much more comfortably fixed than I had supposed and our bed is equal to any hair mattress. I superintended the making of it immediately on my arrival, and think it worth describing. We have first a long pen made airtight with mud and just wide enough for two,—in the pen we placed a layer of thick pine logs— then a layer of pine bushes—next one of straw and finally our beds and blankets.

Gen. Stuart received me very cordially and remarked how glad he was at last to have me on his staff. I thought from what he said, that he got me the position more as a means of getting me on his staff than for any assistance I might give the Engineer Corps.

Tom Price is here in the same department as myself, though ranking as a first lieutenant.[24] He seems to know very little more about it than myself.

I think you had better send at once for my horses as the Spring Campaign will soon commence and I could not then do without them.

Brig. Gen. Wade Hampton. Hampton eventually succeeded to command of the cavalry after Stuart's death. He eventually rose to the rank of lieutenant general.

Brig. Gen. Fitzhugh Lee was the nephew of Gen. Robert E. Lee. A fine cavalry general in his own right, he replaced Hampton in command of the Cavalry Corps in January 1865.

Mr. Blackford is, I am sure, perfectly willing to let me use one of his as long as he can possibly get along without, but Comet is still suffering terribly with his wound and almost useless, and both the others are too miserably poor to stand hard riding without relief. I find nearly all the staff officers have two horses and they say it is impossible to accompany the Gen. on his expeditions without them. Sam will perhaps be best suited to bring them and I want Miranda and either Brenda, Bostona or Kate's mare as you choose. Bostona would probably be best spared, as the other two are ladies horses and pretty good matches besides.

If you cannot get transportation in the cars I think Davidson had best try and get a pack saddle from the Quartermaster in Abingdon, or have one made and send about two hundred pounds of corn along with them. He will find it impossible to get corn along the latter part of his journey. Mr. B. thinks he had better start with only enough to do him to Lynchburg and then buy sufficient to bring him here. He says he will write to his Father, so that if Sam finds any difficulty in getting it [in Lynchburg], he can apply to him—he also thinks he had better rest there a day or two. He need only bring one halter and one old bridle and saddle for himself. Mr. B. is very anxious to buy ___ [word illegible, but is the name of a horse], & desired me to ask that he may have the refusal of her, in case you think of selling—he also wishes to buy a good work horse for his wagon if you can spare one. Mr. B. has been suffering considerably with a bad cold: but is better. He sends his love to all. Give my love to all & believe me

> Your affec. son, Frank
> Tell Kate to write.

Please send at once for the horses, or let me know what other plan would suit better.

Four days later on March 7 he wrote further concerning his need for the horses:

I wrote to you last Tuesday asking you to send at once for my horses, but having heard nothing from you since, I fear my letter miscarried. I did not wait as long as you suggested because I found Mr. Blackford's horse in such a condition as to render it almost impossible for him to spare me the use of one. Comet is almost worthless from his wound and the other two are mere skin and bones and would require constant relief in a march. I will therefore need my horses as soon as they can be brought down [from Abingdon]. It is thought here the Gen. will soon be on the move and if he does before I get my horses, I don't know how I shall manage. I want Miranda and any other you may deem suitable.

So far I have been perfectly well and if we remain in our present camp a few weeks longer, have little doubt of remaining so. I spend the nights as warm and comfortably as if at home and as long as that continues, have little fear of being knocked up again.

Mr. B. has had me busy on a map of the Battle of Fredericksburg for the last few days and I succeed much better than I anticipated. I however wound up with a huge red blot to day while designating the position of troops, making it appear as if Gen. Lee had massed about half his army in a very safe out-of-the-way place....

Give my love to Kate and tell her she might have written—ask her to get me three or four large silk handkerchiefs if she can find them, & have them by the time I come down.

Kate finally did write to her somewhat homesick but very proud brother, and he took time to reply on March 13:

Your long expected letter reached me today. I really began to be seriously alarmed lest your obdurate and most susceptible heart had at last succumbed to Loves keen shaft. I could not imagine what else but a severe case of smite could so long withhold your scribbling propensities, and to be candid, I still believe that something of that sort has happened. Who can it be? I am sure you will tell me, for unless it is our big cousin, I am at a loss to guess and he is or was engaged a few months ago however.

I have been hard at work (that is, in comparison with the other members of the Staff) for the past week on a Map of the Battle of Fredericksburg and much to my delight, put on the finishing touches this evening. I consider it quite a masterpiece and am quite anxious to have a display of it. I am thinking seriously of riding over to Gen. Lee's HeadQuarters in the morning and showing it to him. I am confident that if he is a man of taste as reported, he would make me a Col. of Engrs. without delay. I promised to send Lou Johnston my first attempt at a map, but unfortunately I succeeded so well that Mr. Blackford refused to part with it....

Mr. Blackford and myself rode down to Fredericksburg yesterday it was my first visit there and I find the town even more shattered than I had anticipated. Some of the houses were mere wrecks and I suppose there were fifty that would average 50 cannon shots apiece. We rode along the bank of the river for about half a mile and had a fine view of the Yankee sentinels on the other side about 100 yards off. One of them called and asked Mr. B. if he had paid for that coat (his Yankee overcoat). Mr. B. told him, Yes, he had bought it with a bullet. Talking has been prohibited, but is still carried on to some extent. From Lee's Hill we had a magnificent view of the whole Yankee camp—with Mr. B.'s field glass, we could see accurately everything that was going on—in one place we saw an eight horse battery drilling and in another several squadrons of cavalry, and so distinctly as to distinguish the colors of the horses and the white spots about them. With the naked eye they appeared to be dark masses moving about, with no distinguishable features to denote their nature.

My love to Ma and tell her I should like to have some dried fruit if she can have some sent from home. We have nothing in the world but beef and flour for rations and something in the way of vegetables would be very acceptable.

Years later Robertson recalled:

I greatly feared another collapse, but, strange to say, this rough, half-fed life seemed to be just what was needed for, in spite of the unanimous verdict of the wise M. D.'s of the Medical Board, I throve apace and was soon as tough and rugged as any of my comrades. My 'pericarditis' bothered me only at times. Most of the winter was occupied in mapping or plotting off the Chief Engineer's notes of picket lines, etc.

The Engineer Department of the cavalry staff came near being obliterated on one of our trips. Captain Blackford, Tom Price, myself and three couriers were surveying the picket line along the Rappahannock River. It was a narrow stream at this point, perhaps not more than fifty yards wide. We rode single file and, missing the path, we debouched from the dense brush and suddenly appeared before a badly scared Yankee picket of about a hundred on the opposite bank of the river. As one after another of us rode into the little flat in their front, they evidently thought an attack was intended and all hands rushed into their breastworks and leveled their guns upon us. We at once felt that all depended upon a cool indifference, and that any flurry or attempt to retreat would be fatal. So we six rode quietly along in their front, so near we could distinguish faces; we expected every moment a volley would wipe out the outfit. Picket firing had long since been abandoned by mutual consent as being useless and annoying to all concerned, so Johnny Reb and the Yank simply sat and watched each other and not infrequently made little social exchanges of sentiments, as well as of coffee and tobacco.

3

Germanna Ford

Frank Robertson had been trying to fight the Yankees for two years. His first military outfit, "The Sons of Liberty," had disbanded after a brief campaign without firing a shot, and his father had taken him out of the Richmond Howitzers. He had unceremoniously decamped from the Virginia Military Institute in quest of combat, joined the 48th Virginia Infantry in time to go on the ill-starred expedition into what is now West Virginia only to be declared physically unfit for further military duty, and had yet to undergo his baptism of fire. But now, at last, his strength restored, he had been able to "jine the cavalry," J. E. B. Stuart's cavalry—and he was eager to experience that glorious good time Stuart promised his followers. He would not have long to wait. Almost half a century later Robertson wrote about Virginia in April 1863.

Captain Blackford being sick Captain [Charles R.] Collins[1] of the 15th Virginia Cavalry was temporarily assigned his duties. He, Lieutenant Tom Price and myself were ordered to Germanna Ford on the Rapidan to superintend the rebuilding of the bridge at that point.[2]

Some eighty mechanics selected from various infantry commands were sent to us under Captain McTier[3] and two other officers were assigned. We had been at this job a week or two when Vespasian Chancellor,[4] one of our couriers, reported that an elderly citizen had just crossed the river and he said Yankees were coming in force along the plank road on the other side. Captain Collins said this could not be so, as our cavalry was picketing the Rappahannock and would have promptly notified us if the Yankees were around. Chancellor said the man was a sensible old fellow and "knew a Yank when he saw him," so I strapped my effects quickly on Miranda and offered to go scout the road. Collins said I might.

Crossing the ford, I told the men working out timber on that side to load their guns and be prepared. All was serene for a mile or more and I had about concluded that our old man was mistaken. I was sitting sideways in my saddle, talking to another old man standing in the door of his cabin, when suddenly he yelled, "Look, look!" I looked, and coming out of the woods into the plank road about 75 yards from me, appeared perhaps a squadron of cavalry.

"Come here, Johnny," "Stop, you d——d Reb," and various similar remarks, accompanied by a rattle of carbines, appealed to me very forcibly, and I hurried back to tell Captain Collins. With the Yanks in full pursuit, my incomparable little mare carried me rapidly away from such courtesies. I crossed the river in plunges,—expecting with this slow progress to be shot in the back ere I could reach the south side. The forty men on the far side hadn't time to recross the river before the rapidly advancing enemy was among them and they surrendered, to a man, but we got the forty men on the near side promptly behind the deep cut leading to the ford. Collins sent me up on a knoll to watch the Yanks.

I was watching this very disagreeable performance of surrender with much interest when the hiss of several bullets called my attention to a long skirmish line issuing from the woods. Common sense should have removed me from my pinnacle earlier. Being the only Reb in sight, I was target for many long distance shots. Seeing it would be fatal to stay any longer, I rode down the hill again, hitched Miranda to a big locust tree behind a small cabin, lay down comfortably behind the stone foundation, about a foot high on the upper side, and watched in comparative safety this little game of war. In the meantime, my position behind the little farm house being known to the Yanks on the hill who had seen me go there, a constant fusillade was directed against it, and I could hear the patter of their

Pvt. Vespasian Chancellor, whose family gave their name to the Wilderness crossroads around which Lee and Hooker fought in early May 1863.

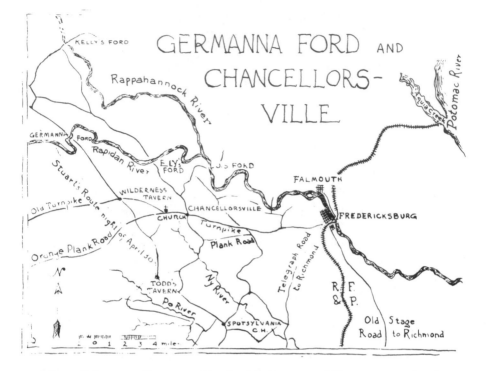

Map of the area between Fredericksburg and Germanna Ford—
the Wilderness.

bullets perforating the walls. A bullet struck just under my face and filled my eyes with stinging dust, so for a brief while I thought they were out, and the exciting maneuvers across the river were unseen.

When I could see again, our forty poor fellows on the opposite side had been marched to the rear, and our forty men in the road cut had not fired a shot. A gaily appointed and very splendid regiment of blue cavalry came dancing down the road opposite. I was very much impressed by their shiny, fully equipped appearance as they rode slowly down upon our forty men in the road-cut. They evidently believed that our bridge-builders had departed,—sad mistake. They had just reached the opposite pier of the bridge when forty muskets rang out and the entire front of this glittering regiment collapsed, and the balance made tracks back up the hill. Our mechanics certainly knew how to shoot and that volley was worthy of record.

These were the first men I had ever seen killed in battle, and it was my first realization of the tragedy of war. No other troops ventured down the road for several hours: our little squad held up the advance of Hooker's main column [of the right wing, including two army corps]. General Lee was most complimentary in his orders on the subject.[5]

After fully five thousand men had deployed on the opposite hills and artillery appeared, our brave little army of forty raised the white flag, as it was impossible to escape up the hill under such a fire as they knew they would be subjected to.[6]

The firing had ceased for some minutes when a man ran around the corner of my protecting house and announced that we had surrendered. This was my first experience in the cavalry and my heart sank within me when I thought of Miranda being ridden by some Yankee while her master was tied up in prison. It occurred to me that she might yet escape, so I unbuckled my belt and hung my pistol and sabre on the cantle of the saddle, intending to turn Miranda loose, hoping she would retreat to the rear and be taken by some one other than a Yank. I was just about to start her up the hill when the absolute quiet seemed to urge me to go with her. It was fully 250 yards ere I could top the hill and it would have been an absolute impossibility had the host of Yanks in range been on the alert. The mare was fast I knew, but I also knew that bullets were faster, and I fully realized that my chances were slight.

The poor soldier who was with me (I don't recall his name), when he saw me rebuckle my belt on, asked me what I was going to do. I said, "I'm going to try to get over the hill. I'll not surrender!" His appealing look I shall never forget. He was also crazy to get away. He left at a run as I started. I suppose I had gone half way up the hill when the first shots were heard: my companion fell. Then the rattle increased and, lying flat in the saddle, I saw dust flying around me. Well, over the crest I went safe and sound, and never in my life have I felt better.

Captain Collins and Lieutenant Price also got away safely, as did three men who were cutting wood back of Germanna. The small group of survivors joined together south of the river. "We retreated slowly before the Yankee advance guard, notifying people along the road what was coming, and thereby creating many hasty departures of the panicked people from their homes." But Robertson could not stay away from the sight of his first "battle" and returned there late in May 1863. He reminisced years later:

I was again at Germanna some three weeks later and the old woman who lived across the river from our camp told me that the Yankees had buried ten of their men who were killed in the first volley and carried off a lot of wounded. She also told me of the poor soldier who had tried to follow me: her husband had counted three bullet holes in his back, and he had been buried where he fell. So far as I know, this was the only one of our men who was killed. In the small house I was protected by, I counted twenty-nine bullet holes. Miranda would surely have been killed several times, so to speak, but for the big locust tree she was tied to and which stood immediately back of the house.

Or as he wrote his father on May 30:

> I learned from a man who lives on this side the river and whose house was occupied by Yankee General [Brig. Gen. Alpheus S.] Williams,[7] that they had five thousand men engaged,[8] before we evacuated and that their loss was five killed and ten wounded. We lost one killed and I saw the poor fellows grave as I passed by nearly in the exact spot where I dropped my sabre.

Did "a brave little army" of less than a hundred Confederates really delay the Twelfth Army Corps of the United States that 29th day of April, 1863? Northern authorities do not agree as to the exact number of the enemy (their estimates range from "about fifty" to "one hundred and fifty"), but they do admit that a handful of Rebels held up more than ten thousand men of the Twelfth Army Corps (13,457, to be exact), as well as the Eleventh (12,977) just behind, not to mention the 6th New York Cavalry (estimated at about 600). These organizations, together with the Fifth Army Corps (which was to cross at Ely's Ford), made up the right wing of the Army of the Potomac, under the command of Major General Henry W. Slocum.[9]

This right wing had begun to cross the Rappahannock at 4 o'clock that morning. The cavalry regiment led the way and was constantly, if lightly, engaged with the Confederate cavalry. They took a number of pickets prisoner and, more importantly, intercepted the couriers sent to warn the men at the fords. When they first discovered the Confederate detachment at Germanna, the 6th New York Cavalry "...dismounted and engaged the enemy on foot until our infantry came up...."[10]

Brigadier General Thomas H. Ruger[11] was in command of the advance guard, consisting of the Third Brigade of the First Division of the Twelfth Corps. About 11 A.M., when he reached a point about two miles north of Germanna Ford he heard from scouts of the 6th New York Cavalry that there was a detachment of about 150 Confederates at the ford, engaged in building a bridge. An hour later, having advanced something more than a mile, he received "orders to deploy as skirmishers on both sides of the road and advance rapidly...."[12]

Like the good soldier that he was, General Ruger obeyed his orders meticulously. He deployed the 2nd Massachusetts Infantry to the right of the road, and the 3rd Wisconsin to the left. Between them marched the 27th Indiana, with two pieces from the 1st Maine Field Artillery. The 13th New Jersey and the 107th New York, being made up of unseasoned troops, followed the deployed regiments in columns of fours. There was, of course, no reason for taking any chances against a band of perhaps one hundred and fifty determined Rebels!

The Yankees never did admit that the Confederates had only eighty men in this skirmish. "The number of prisoners on both banks," the official record showed, "aggregated 105, of whom 7 were officers." It would appear that the 6th New York Cavalry captured about 25 Rebels on their march to the ford. Colonel William Hawley,[13] commanding the 3rd Wisconsin Infantry on the left flank of the advance, said that in the exchange of shots, his men killed a Confederate and wounded three more; a captain and 23 men surrendered. Colonel Samuel M. Quincy,[14] commanding the 2nd Massachusetts Infantry, reported that his skirmishers surrounded a house on the north bank and captured 30 Rebels without a shot being fired; then they opened on the cut in the road. "On their way to the rear [the prisoners] gave frequent vent to their astonishment at the thousands of men they passed, showing the Federal movement had been executed without knowledge of the enemy."[15] The Union commanders were very proud of their excellent security, particularly since the Confederates had so long been kept accurately informed of their plans well in advance. The Confederates also could be proud of their brief but heroic stand in the face of overwhelming numbers, and Robertson had finally had his baptism of fire.

As much as his escape brought joy and exhilaration to Robertson the Yankees were not the only cause for worry the young engineer had that April:

> While at Germanna my servant boy Sam was ill with pneumonia. There was no doctor with our command so I rode fourteen miles to see one who had just had his arm taken off. Though he was suffering great pain, when I told him of Sam's condition, he told me where to find his bottle of fly blister and how to apply it. Sam was very ill,—delirious—and I had no one to help me. I spent four nights with him in a half torn down cabin in the pine woods, with no bed, no light, no medicine. The last night I was with him he became sane. Next day Mr. Hooker's little raid sent me off to Chancellorsville, and Sam was looked after by a Mr. Gay on whose place he was. Seven weeks after, he walked into our house in Rich-

mond. He had nursed me through camp fever on Valley Mountain, and this was a return of the compliment, though I must modestly admit, take oath indeed, that Sam had the better nurse of the two. That I weathered the fever under the conditions was strange; that I lived through Sam's nursing is a miracle.

Robertson had already experienced a couple of miracles during his short period of service, and he would continue to encounter them as the war continued. His next one would take place on the battle-field of Chancellorsville.

4

Chancellorsville

Soon after the Battle of Fredericksburg in December 1862, General Ambrose E. Burnside was replaced by "Fighting Joe" Hooker as commander of the Army of the Potomac.[1] Hooker, a graduate of West Point, class of 1837, and a veteran of the Mexican War, had resigned from the Army as a brevet lieutenant colonel on February 21, 1853 to seek his fortune in California. He had not been very successful. At the outbreak of the war he felt it his duty to hurry to Washington to offer his services again, but he had difficulty in raising money to get across the continent. Once he reached the capital he faced another problem. During the Mexican War he had made certain critical remarks about General Winfield Scott, and upon his arrival in the nation's capital he learned that "Old Fuss and Feathers" had a long memory. Scott did not welcome him back into the fold, nor facilitate his meeting the president. When Hooker finally did secure an interview with the commander-in-chief a few days after the First Battle of Manassas, they began to talk about that disastrous defeat. "I can say, without vanity, Mr. President," remarked Hooker, "that I am a damned sight better general than any you had on that field." This display of self-confidence, it is said, so delighted Mr. Lincoln, that he promptly appointed Hooker one of his first Brigadier Generals of Volunteers.

Hooker took command of the Army of the Potomac at a time when its morale was appallingly low. Eighty-five thousand officers and men were absent, and there were some two hundred desertions a day.[2] Confederate spies were everywhere, and they were getting their messages to General Lee. On the other hand, the Union generals were receiving practically no intelligence about Lee's army.

By the middle of April General Hooker had renewed the army's spirit, tightened its security, as has been noted, and made considerable progress in rounding up information as to the Army of Northern Virginia. An optimist, and rightly so by virtue of the men and material at his command, he planned an "On to Richmond" campaign that he expected would insure victory and end the war. He planned well. (No less an authority than Stonewall Jackson[3] called it "an excellent plan.") Thus by April 30, 1863, Hooker had succeeded in assembling his army where he wanted it—south of the Rapidan and Rappahannock rivers.

Two days earlier, on Tuesday evening, April 28, General Lee learned from Stuart's scouts that Federal troops were moving in great force towards Kelly's Ford on the Rappahannock. The next day he was informed that the enemy was wading the Rapidan at Germanna and at Ely's Fords. On Thursday, the last day of April, John Sedgwick with the Sixth Corps crossed the Rappahannock by pontoon bridges three miles south of Fredericksburg.[4] By nightfall Hooker's entire army of 130,000 men was south of the rivers. Only at Germanna had they been delayed. This time the Confederates did not know in advance where the Yankees would attempt to cross or even when, so they were unable to put up stiff resistance anywhere. Hooker's "On to Richmond" campaign had begun.

Chancellorsville is about ten miles west of Fredericksburg. As the crow flies, the distance is somewhat shorter. For the foot-soldier with his lumbering wagon trains and artillery, particularly when harassed by men who knew the Wilderness, the ten miles was immeasurably longer. Chancellorsville was not a town, not even a village. Five miles west and a little north, the road from Culpeper across Germanna Ford joins the turnpike from Orange. Three miles east of this point the Orange Plank Road becomes one with the pike for two miles, and then, at Chancellorsville, leaves it to swerve sharply southeast, seemingly an extension of yet another road from Ely's and the United States fords on the north. The turnpike and the Orange Plank Road join again four and a half miles to the east as they continue on to Fredericksburg. Chancellorsville, though an important road junction near which stood the great Chancellor mansion and its outbuildings, was in short just a clearing in the Wilderness of Spotsylvania County.

This Wilderness covers about three hundred square miles, some fifteen miles from north to south and about twenty miles from west to east. Scrubby second-growth timber from charcoal choppings or heavier stands of pine and oak with dense and tangled undergrowth would impede the progress of troops, as would the swamps and sluggish streams.

On this May Day of 1863, the Yankee troops were in high good humor as they marched along the turnpike and the Orange Plank Road. Their commanding general had assured them only the day before that all roads led to victory: "Our enemy must either ingloriously fly or come out from behind his intrenchments and give us battle on our own ground, where certain destruction awaits him."[5]

As subordinates, Hooker had George G. Meade, Henry W. Slocum, Oliver O. Howard, John Sedgwick, and Darius Couch, and they had more than twice as many men under them as the Confederates.[6] But the veteran Army of Northern Virginia was commanded by Robert E. Lee, who had Stonewall Jackson, James Longstreet, J. E. B. Stuart, A. P. Hill, and lesser officers of the same fine clay: Richard "Dick" Anderson, Jubal Early, William Dorsey Pender, Sam McGowan, and Edward Porter Alexander.[7] The Confederate men in the ranks had known combat, weariness, and privation. Hardened veterans of earlier campaigns, some of them had followed the roads and paths of the Wilderness from boyhood. Nearly all were afraid, but they were ready. A few longed for the fierceness of battle.

The small bridge building expedition that had included Capt. Collins, Lt. Price, and Assistant Engineer Robertson had gotten in the way of one of Hooker's columns at Germanna Ford. The three officers and their few companions continued their retreat on the evening of April 29. The next day they joined Lee's army south and east of Chancellorsville. Robertson remembered:

> Things were lively in the cavalry division that day. Staff and couriers were kept busy. Three of us were sent through a dense cedar and pine covered hill to see what we could find. We rode square into a Yankee party—apparently on a similar errand—a brief skirmish with pistols and, being largely outnumbered, we beat a retreat. Miranda chose this occasion to practice her famous backing feat, which had dismounted sundry riders. My saddle girth broke, and saddle and myself went over her head. The back strap held, and I pitched the saddle back and jumped on,—leaving my beautiful red saddle blan-

kets on the ground. I did not think it judicious to tarry to pick them up. The Yanks must have also retreated as we saw nothing more of this scouting party.

That night Stuart, accompanied by Major Johann August Heinrich Heros von Borcke[8] and two or three others, left Todd's Tavern by the light of the new moon to ride to Spotsylvania Court House, where they expected to find General Lee. On the way they ran into the 6th New York Cavalry under the command of Lt. Col. Duncan McVicar. A brisk but confused little skirmish ensued. The 3rd and 5th Virginia Cavalry Regiments rescued General Stuart. Colonel McVicar was killed in the encounter.[9]

About daybreak, May 1, Stuart rode in at Lee's headquarters where he reported that he had detached two regiments under Rooney Lee[10] to watch the Federal cavalry under Gen. George Stoneman who had been sent by Hooker to cut the Richmond, Fredericksburg, and Potomac Railroad in Lee's rear.[11] Hooker expected Lee to send, if not his whole army, at least all his cavalry to intercept Stoneman, but the Confederate leader kept most of his cavalry in the neighborhood of Chancellorsville where he utilized it effectively. In view of Hooker's brilliant opening of the campaign, it is the consensus of military historians that the lack of adequate cavalry was an important factor in his defeat. Still, Lee's situation that morning seemed desperate with Hooker on the north, Sedgwick on the east, and Stoneman between him and Richmond. Outnumbered and outgunned, what could he do? One of the first things he did was to violate

Brig. Gen. William Henry Fitzhugh "Rooney" Lee was the son of Robert E. Lee. He was severely wounded at the Battle of Brandy Station and later attained the rank of major general.

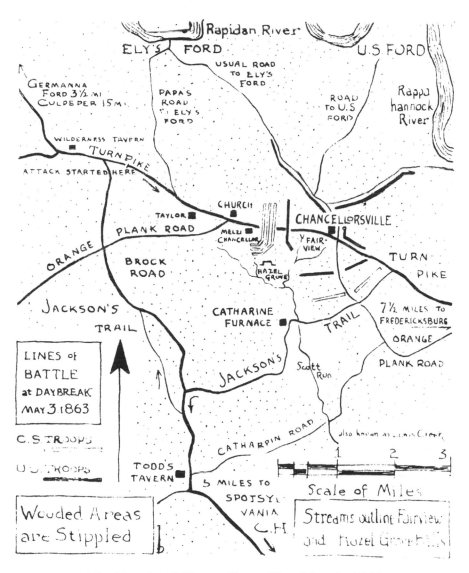

The Battle of Chancellorsville - May 3, 1863.

the classic military maxim and divide his army in the presence of
the enemy. He left Early with ten thousand men at Fredericksburg
to hold Sedgwick and his Sixth Corps, and Lee with the rest turned
to attend to Hooker.

That first day of May 1863 opened with skirmishing all along
the line. Thousands of Confederate foot-soldiers were on the march
before dawn. By 4 P.M. Jackson had driven from the east on the

Plank Road to within a mile of Chancellorsville, and General
Ambrose R. Wright was only a mile and a half away on the turnpike.[12] Jackson wanted Wright to edge off from the left flank and
attack Chancellorsville from Catherine Furnace, a mile and a half
south and a bit west. Before ordering this attack, he joined Stuart
to inspect the ground. The party was fired on by Federal artillery,
and General Stuart said to General Jackson, "General Jackson, we
must move from here." Robertson reported the incident in his reminiscences:

> Near the Furnace, we (General Stuart and staff) were behind a
> battery of Beckham's horse artillery.[13] It was a four gun battery and
> was pushed forward on a hill in the woods, and it opened fire on the
> Yanks entrenched at Chancellorsville. Six Federal batteries, we
> learned afterwards, and we believed it afterwards, were command-
> ing the hill and they promptly replied to our fire. Such a storm of
> shot and shell came down upon us that an immediate retreat was in
> order. I don't know the name of the battery, but heard it lost 56 men
> killed and wounded, and every horse in a few minutes.[14] The Yanks
> evidently suspected that our troops would occupy the hill, and they
> had figured out a perfect range for it.
> It was here that Channing Price, an old Richmond school-mate of
> mine, was shot through the leg.[15] He was General Stuart's Adjutant
> General, and he was a fine boy in all respects. We were standing
> together when he was hit and I helped him on his horse. Some hours
> later, and ignorant of his true condition, I sat on his couch [he had
> been moved to the home of Colonel Charles C. Wellford in the neigh-
> borhood] and we talked and laughed for some time,—I saying I wished
> I had his nice little wound and he saying, "I wish you had." Suddenly
> he began to talk wild and I went over to Dr. [Talcott] Eliason (our
> staff M.D.)[16] and told him that Channing was delirious. He simply
> remarked, "He will be dead in fifteen minutes."
> We had no tourniquets to stop the flow of blood, and afterwards
> General Stuart gave one to each of his staff. Mine is still in my car-
> tridge box. Modern surgery with proper appliances would doubtless
> have saved him and two others.

Toward sundown Jackson sent word to Lee that the enemy had
checked his advance, and a little later Lee joined his subordinate
to plan the next move. As they were talking, Stuart rode up with
good news from Fitz Lee. The Yankee right flank was in the air,[17]
and could be turned if it could be reached. Stuart galloped off to
see if there was a road westward that lay beyond the Federal outposts. Before midnight Lee and Jackson had agreed to attack
Hooker's right from the west.

Maj. Richard Channing Price, Stuart's assistant adjutant general, who was mortally wounded on May 1, 1863. He was greatly mourned by Stuart and the staff.

During the night Stuart found a chaplain who had lived in the neighborhood and sent him to Jackson with information as to a possible route. Jackson thought the road he proposed too close to the enemy lines, so he sent the preacher with his trusted map-maker, Major Jed Hotchkiss, to inquire of Colonel [Charles Carter] Wellford if there were a better one.[18] They returned with word that Wellford had recently opened such a road to enable him to haul cordwood and iron ore to his furnace. Lee then gave Jackson his final instructions, telling him that Stuart would cover his movement with cavalry. They held their last conference just after dawn, and then Jackson's column, six miles long, swept into the forest.

While the three divisions of Jackson's Second Army Corps, "Old Stonewall's Army," engaged in the difficult task of moving through the Wilderness of Spotsylvania, the fourteen thousand men who had been left with Lee kept up a great, if simulated, show of strength under the direction of Maj. Gen. Richard H. Anderson and Maj. Gen. Lafayette McLaws.[19]

During the morning of May 2 Jackson and his toiling column had an unexpected stroke of luck. Just before the Federal outposts saw and reported this mass movement of enemy troops, their route had turned south for a short distance on the Brock Road. And so it was that the already overconfident Hooker was quick to conclude that Lee's army had begun to "ingloriously fly." In front of

Jackson's column was the 1st Virginia Cavalry, Fitz Lee command-ing. In his later years Robertson remembered the ride vividly:

> We moved out promptly with Jackson's infantry following, head-ing for Hooker's rear. Our cavalry being off in all directions, General Stuart and his staff seemed alone in the wilderness.
>
> We crossed the Plank Road and ascended a hill to the Chancellorsville pike halting there under a big oak tree. Almost im-mediately General Stuart ordered me to ride back along the road we had come to meet General Jackson and tell him, "Our cavalry have driven off the Yankee cavalry and there seem to be few of the enemy about." I soon met Old Jack riding with his staff ahead of his toiling infantry. The men were moving at their best gait, which is at best discouragingly slow. The only reply vouch-safed my message was, "Give General Stuart my thanks."
>
> General Jackson impressed me as looking more like a preacher on his ride to his death than ever before. He looked like a supremely grave divine on his way to church, and no stranger would have sus-pected the wonderful influence he exerted over those poor half-fed and ragged troops that followed him. They looked tired, but they were swinging along in fine spirits. He was surely marching his men that day.

By 2 o'clock in the afternoon, though his rear brigades were six miles back, at least four hours off, Jackson had himself reached the Plank Road. Here he was met by Fitz Lee, who invited him to the top of a neighboring hill to look down upon a sight more pleas-ing than a soldier's fairest dream. What the two men saw from the top of their hill was the Eleventh Corps of the Army of the Potomac! Maj. Gen. Oliver O. Howard's troops were smoking, playing cards, cooking, sleeping, all unaware of how precarious their situation had become. Fitz Lee recommended, however, that Jackson should advance to the old turnpike, and Jackson accepted the advice of his junior officer who was more familiar with the ground.

By the middle of the afternoon the head of Jackson's column, which in the morning had been on Hooker's left, was well behind his right. Soon the divisions would be up. Even after they had arrived and 28,000 men had been deployed in the woods, almost within hailing distance of the Union line, no Federal commander of rank appeared to suspect any danger. This is the more remark-able in that many reports of the Confederate flanking movement had been brought in since Jackson's men had left Catharine Fur-nace, but the officers who received these reports considered them too ridiculous to pass on. The recollection continues:

After reporting to my General I went across the road to inspect some Yankee prisoners, and was talking to a cavalry captain when Jackson's column debouched from the weeds. The Yank gazed at them in astonishment and asked what it meant. I told him it was "Old Jack and his men." He replied, "I guess Uncle Joe Hooker will have to wade the Rappahannock tonight."

This splendid body of men—bright muskets and ragged uniforms—were at once formed in line of battle, [Brig. Gen. Robert E.] Rodes' division in the van, then [Maj. Gen. Issac R.] Trimble's under [Brig. Gen. Raleigh E.] Colston, with [Maj. Gen.] A. P. Hill's in the rear, astride the old turnpike, at right angles to it.[20] Skirmishers were thrown forward and all lay down as the different regiments came into formation.

While this was in progress, General Stuart and General Jackson were sitting on their horses conversing. General Stuart sent Lieutenant [Walter Q.] Hullihen[21] and myself to see "what was in front." We rode through Jackson's line of skirmishers—keeping in the thick brush along side the road. I suppose we had gone two hundred yards beyond the skirmishers when we decided to go to the edge of the road and see what we could see. Hullihen was climbing a sapling and I was standing in my saddle, both looking down the road where we could see the wheels of a battery and artillerymen at their posts. Just then I looked across the road: diagonally, not fifty yards away, were standing three Yanks, guns in hand, staring stupidly at us. Why these Yanks neither challenged nor shot is one of the mysteries to be solved. They may have been foreigners,[22]—certainly they were damned fools. They were evidently in the advance skirmish line and we could hardly have been more than thirty yards from its extension on our side of the road. Hullihen slid down his tree into the saddle and I slipped into mine, and we went back to report. The Generals were still talking when we reported, and we lay down to watch the proceedings. The tense silence seemed ominous and uncanny.

By now it was nearly six o'clock. Since early morning Jackson's men had marched some twelve miles through the Wilderness of Spotsylvania and had taken up their battle positions. Jackson sat silent on Little Sorrel. Major Eugene Blackford, Frank's old companion in athletics at the University, now in command of Rodes' splendidly trained skirmishers, reported that the skirmish line was fully extended and ready to go forward. Old Jack raised his right hand as a signal to advance. The next few hours were never forgotten by Robertson:

> Beginning at the road and running down the battle line on each side until lost to hearing, the word, "Forward" was given in many varied tones. It was the last word no doubt that many in those ranks

ever heard. The awful silence was broken by the most terrible musketry of the Civil War. There must have been artillery on the enemy's
side, but I heard nothing but the Confederate yell as Jackson's men
rushed forward. The Yanks made a hasty getaway, nor halted a moment until they reached their heavy entrenchments at
Chancellorsville, about two miles, I judge, from the point of attack.

General Stuart and staff rode down the road keeping in line with
the advance, but met no opposition except long distance attentions.
Firing slackened after dark. The General summoned me and asked
if I recalled a certain road leading north from the turnpike, and told
me to report to Colonel [James H.] Drake[23] of the 1st Virginia Cavalry, and show it to him. My recollections of that road were surely
vague, but I thought it better to look for the road rather than tell
General Stuart I didn't know where the road was. We of the junior
staff had discovered that he had little patience with any of us who
didn't know, so I found the 1st Virginia and reported to Colonel Drake.
He evidently didn't know me as one of General Stuart's staff and addressed me as "guide."

"Well, guide, show me the road."

Colonel Drake's language did not fall lightly on the ears of that
unhappy and ignorant "guide." It was pitch dark and the Colonel
and myself rode back at the head of the regiment to take this mysterious road. The first opening in the thick woods to the right I desig-
nated as the road. The 1st Virginia disappeared down this
tree-enveloped highway, and I returned to General Stuart, considering muchly where Colonel Drake and his regiment were going through
the scrub brush, dark as Hades. General Stuart gave me no opportunity to express my doubts about that road and I was not happy when
I thought perhaps "guide" had misguided that regiment. I never heard
anything more however, on the subject of the road.

Shortly after returning to General Stuart, he, staff and couriers,
followed by a big North Carolina infantry regiment [the 16th], apparently followed Colonel Drake down that same road, but it was very
dark, and it may have been another. The one we followed led to Ely's
Ford [across the Rapidan] where we found [Brigadier General William W.] Averell's cavalry in camp and doubtless feeling very good and
secure around their far-to-the-rear camp fires.[24] We halted on the
edge of a deep hollow and the North Carolina infantry passed us and
deployed along the ravine. Opposite we could see the Averell camp
fires, tents and long lines of horses tied up Yankee fashion to heavy
stretches of well braced rope. From the hilarious sounds we judged
the Averell horsemen were enjoying life. The North Carolinians
stealthily crawled upon the unsuspecting camp, and we could scarcely
hear more than slight rustling of the brush and leaves as they crawled
forward.

While we sat looking and listening to this boisterous and overhappy camp, two staff officers dashed up and immediately interviewed General Stuart. I heard one of them say, "General Jackson has been shot and you are wanted." General Stuart called his staff together at once, and ordered Major von Borcke, his chief of staff, to remain and take charge of the troops we had with us, and to "keep Robertson with you." He and the rest of the staff rode off towards Chancellorsville where he at once assumed command of Jackson's Corps at Jackson's request.[25]

Watching this camp with its numerous fires, long lines of regularly pitched tents and hitched horses, my interest became tense as I waited for the grand wake-up we were about to give them. Suddenly the whole front blazed with the crash of a regimental volley, and in an instant utter confusion prevailed. Songs became shrieks of agony or terror. We could see men rushing from their tents, horses breaking away, running down tents, scattering fires. Panic was supreme. Pending this happy condition, our lines retired and all hands marched back towards Chancellorsville. Von and myself, the show being over, did the same.

We could not find General Stuart. Von Borcke and myself spent the balance of the night behind a big pine tree. Shells were searching the woods and they kept one from being sleepy.

With Jackson seriously wounded and A. P. Hill at least temporarily incapacitated, the responsibility for more than half of the Army of Northern Virginia had come to rest upon the shoulders of the man who had gathered news for Lee, a thirty-year-old cavalryman whose only real experience at directing infantry in action occurred at Dranesville, Virginia, on December 20, 1861, when he commanded four regiments in a brief skirmish with Federal forces.[26] Nor did this young cavalryman have a general officer under him who before that day had ever led a division in battle. His own scattered staff was hardly big enough for the control of the cavalry division, and they neither knew the commanders of the infantry divisions, nor were known by them. Of Jackson's staff, only Major Sandy Pendleton reported to Stuart that night, and he knew little of the terrain and nothing of his old chief's plans. Moreover, the leading divisions had gotten hopelessly tangled up, and there was strong resistance facing the Confederate right flank, where Maj. Gen. Daniel E. Sickles and Brig. Gen. Alfred Pleasonton[27] had gone out the morning before to investigate those Rebels bearing south; indeed, Sickles had attempted a counter-attack while Stuart was at Ely's Ford.

James Ewell Brown Stuart was undaunted. He and Jackson had a close friendship. Often Stuart had joked with that stern Christian soldier as few had ever dared. Now Jackson was entrusting him with his corps and the fate of the army.

Stuart spent a busy night with no moment's rest learning where his troops were. On the extreme right, James J. Archer's Brigade faced almost due south, toward Hazel Grove.[28] Next was Samuel McGowan and then James Lane, whose left flank rested on the turnpike; Lane's Brigade faced east.[29] Just north of the road were the troops of Dorsey Pender and Edward L. Thomas, and they also faced east, towards Chancellorsville, a little more than a mile away.[30] All of these brigades of Hill's Division were, because of General Hill's injury the evening before, under the command of General Harry Heth, a stranger to most of the officers and men.[31]

As Stuart had ordered, the attack was launched at dawn. On the right Archer pushed forward and seized Hazel Grove, capturing four guns. Had he only known it, Hooker had already ordered the withdrawal of the troops occupying this site, and Archer could have had it without fighting for it half an hour later. Stuart, realizing that Hazel Grove was the key position, devoted his personal attention to the hill, promptly moving in horse artillery. McGowan and those north of him, in their initial rush, overwhelmed the first line of the Federal defense and reached the second, only to be driven back by the Northern infantry. During the advance, contact between Archer and McGowan was lost, and the enemy was quick to exploit this half-moon-like gap. By 7 A.M. that morning, though Archer still held Hazel Grove, McGowan's Brigade was on the reverse side of the first line of Union fortifications, and content to stay there. Stuart ordered General Raleigh Colston, in command of Jackson's old division, to send re-inforcements, and he sent the Stonewall Brigade and another from the Valley, recently commanded by Col. John Arthur Campbell, at that moment under the command of Col. Thomas S. Garnett.[32]

These fresh troops passed through McGowan's men, "the first volunteers of the Palmetto State," men who had won imperishable laurels on many other battlefields. The Virginians pressed to within seventy yards of the second line only to be driven back too,—not at all to the discomfiture of the South Carolina officers who had been working so hard to get their men to charge again—and then the soldiers from the Valley also became content to remain where they were. The Federal infantry who in such stalwart fashion opposed the Rebels in this furious action were mostly of the Third Brigade, First Division, Twelfth Army Corps, under Gen. Thomas Ruger, the same men who had rounded up the Confederate detail at Germanna Ford four days earlier. The 13th New Jersey and the 117th New York could never again be considered unseasoned. It was beginning to look as if Stuart would lose his first infantry battle. Robertson continues his recollection of these events:

> In the morning we found General Stuart hard at work acquaint-ing himself with the positions of the troops he had been so unexpect-edly called upon to command. His staff and couriers were constantly on the go. Early that morning he ordered me, "Go to the front. Find General McGowan. Tell him to hold his own. Reinforcements are coming. Be quick." The firing was very heavy in front and I had no difficulty in knowing the direction. I went quick and was joined by a courier with a dispatch for somebody at the front. He begged me to take his message, but I wanted company then anyway, so I declined.

> The road we followed led directly to the firing line. As we rode through a thicket of small pines, I could hear the snap of the bullets and see the twigs dropping. I was conscious that my only hope was speed and Miranda was making good headway when we suddenly emerged from the thicket. A glance showed me our line of battle down a slope some forty yards before us; the slope had been cleared out to construct Yankee breastworks. Our men were crouched behind this line of heavy breastworks taken from the enemy. Beyond were open oak woods and a fringe of smoke, perhaps 300 yards off, showed the Yankee line of battle. A quick look convinced me that the one and only hope was to fall to the ground and run under the breastworks. Going fast, I rolled some distance on the ground, just fast enough to escape being crushed by my courier's blaze-faced horse. The courier, I suppose, was shot when we first came out of the woods. Miranda reached the breastworks before her rider and lined up behind an oak just back of the works packed with McGowan's men.

> I ran down the line attempting to find General McGowan, yelling in the ears of every officer I found on his feet, for the racket was terrible, and limbs and bark were filling the air. I jumped over a pile of dead men opposite an opening in the works, and at last learned that McGowan had been wounded and sent to the rear. The shell fire was very heavy. I gave my orders to everybody I could. The gap in the breastworks had to be crossed again—dead men piled up there - no doubt a constant stream of bullets going through. I passed the death trap at a run.

> I regard this ride into full view of the Federal battle line as the closest call of my army life, and it will ever be a marvel to me that both Miranda and myself escaped without even a scratch. A cousin of

mine, Tom Trigg, of Abingdon, who was with the troops behind the
works, told me afterwards that he saw me come in on all fours, and
that every mounted man who came out of the thicket had been shot.
He told me also that his regiment, the 37th Virginia Infantry, had
lost fifteen men in crossing that gap in the breastworks.

The Yanks were coming now and our firing growing slack when
out of the woods came the old Stonewall Brigade at a run. I could see
the dust fly from their frowzy jackets and men pitched forward dead
or wounded. As they reached my tree, one tall soldier almost fell on
me with blood spurting from his forehead. He did not move or even
twitch after he fell. Soon after the Stonewall Brigade arrived, I took
Miranda's reins and streaked out along the works for possibly two
hundred yards.

I soon found General Stuart and was with him when he rode in
front of the line I had been with, and ordered the charge.

Just after the General had ordered the charge, he was giving me
orders when a shell or solid shot came so close it knocked me out of
the saddle. It came from the rear and I saw the darned thing going
down the road. It looked like a bee flying from you. I was back in the
saddle almost before the General could ask if I was hurt, but he had
to repeat the message he was giving me. Beyond a headache for some
hours, I seemed none the worse for the "winding" as it was called.[33]

When the charge was made therefore, I was on my way with a
message to General Pender who commanded our left, north of the
road. I had to pass through burning woods filled with wounded from
both sides. Their cries for help resounded through the woods, but the
fire rolled on and over them. Twice I passed through this hell on
earth with orders for General Pender. The second time I reached
him he was spitting blood: a bullet had just passed through the head
of his Adjutant and struck him in the chest.[34] He was a splendid-
looking soldier. He and Rodes and Stuart impressed me as true sons
of Mars. Their appearance on the battlefield was an inspiration in
itself, and death at the front was the reward of each.

The Stonewall Brigade quickly recovered itself, and after General Stuart's plea the men charged as if still under the eye of their old
commander. They fought on until they reached Fairview, but then,
having lost a third of their number and finding themselves alone,
they retreated in good order to the log works.

The fire from the Federal guns began to slacken. For the first
time in the history of the War, their ammunition was running low,
and the last gun was withdrawn from Fairview about 10 o'clock. Actually they had plenty of ammunition south of the rivers, but their
system of distribution had failed.[35] A bit earlier, [Maj. Gen. Richard
H.] Anderson, on the left flank of the small army still under Lee's
immediate command, had fought his way up from Catharine Furnace

a mile to the south, and established contact with Archer. General Lee rode into Hazel Grove while it was still under heavy fire. Calm as usual in the presence of danger, he ordered the reunited army to press on to Chancellorsville from the south, the southwest, and the west, where the troops were still astride the turnpike. The men rushed on irresistibly and joyfully. The battle was drawing to its close.

When the Federal left gave way thousands stampeded across the road. Immediately in the road were two brass howitzers, firing canister at short range into this flowing mass. I never saw gunners serve their pieces with such energy. My old teacher at Hanover Academy, Colonel Hilary Jones[36] of the Artillery, was sitting on his horse, directing the fire of these guns. I sat by him for probably ten minutes watching this performance with intense satisfaction. Though thousands were running across the road, I did not see one stop to fire. Had this stampeded mob paused one moment and fired upon these unprotected guns, we would have been obliterated. Panic makes men little better than beasts. These men seemed interested only in following their leaders. They looked neither to the right nor to the left, but rushed pell mell into the jaws of death. The execution by these two isolated guns was something fearful. The road was quickly piled up with heaps of dead and wounded. One man stood stone dead on one bent knee with his hand uplifted, his mouth wide open. He had stiffened in that attitude, the only thing of this sort I saw in my service in the Confederate Army.

Riding beyond the pile of dead men, I saw a man sitting on the roadside—stark naked and black as a full blood negro. Two little streams of blood trickled down his swollen cheeks from eyes that were forever closed. I paused to look upon this hideous victim of war and learned that he was so stunned that he felt no pain. The strength that enabled him to sit up may have permitted him to live on, certainly blind, probably deaf. That black, eyeless, swollen figure of woe will be ever with me.

With the flight of this corps or division, the battle of Chancellorsville was practically ended, though there continued considerable artillery firing by both sides. The Chancellorsville clearing was in General Lee's possession and Hooker's grand army was in full retreat. The large brick Chancellor house was burning and the field around was covered with the debris of war, many dead men and horses, smashed artillery outfits and caissons, wrecked wagons of all descriptions: the great battle was over.

In after years Robertson recounted some of his other experiences during the battle:

Rather a singular experience was given Major von Borcke and myself. We had gotten behind a big oak while under a terrific artil-

lery fire. He was next to the tree and I was affectionately lying close
to him. We felt a heavy jar, accompanied by smoke, bark and splin-
ters. At first we thought we had been blown to atoms. We did not
know what had happened until on leaving we discovered a disc-shaped
excavation on the trunk of the tree opposite to where we had been. It
was very apparent that a shell had struck and exploded against the
protecting tree.

Our service was so arduous and constant,—General Stuart had a
small staff,—that towards evening my little mare fell twice from exhaustion,—there was no more buck left in her. I too from pure exhaustion and want of food, was as near dead as many of those lying
wounded on the battlefield. Few of General Stuart's followers had
either slept or eaten for two days,—horses ditto. Once I fell asleep
with my head resting on a fence rail. An artillery caisson came by at
a gallop and ran over the other end of the rail, bouncing my head up
violently. I believed that a shell had blown me to pieces and my surprise was exceeding great when I found myself running across the
field unhurt.

That night, the close of two days fighting, was comparatively
quiet,—except for the cries of the many wounded men scattered over
perhaps a square mile. Lieutenant Theodore S. Garnett, Jr.[37] (aide
de camp to General Stuart, and my chum and tent mate) and I crawled
over a fence in the dark and were soon fast asleep. We awoke the
next morning between two ancient graves and immediately at our
head, close enough to touch, was lying a huge Yankee.

The young engineer was greatly impressed by his chief's performance while commanding Jackson's Corps. In his concluding
account of the battle he wrote:

My duties carried me to every part of the field, sometimes following Stuart, but generally carrying messages. General Stuart had to
know all that was going on from the charge of a picket to that of a
corps. He was the embodiment of all that was game. That day he
rode the lines with flashing eyes and heroic courage, exhorting, commanding, inspiring. He seemed tireless, he seemed everywhere. He
was almost always alone, for as soon as a staff officer appeared, he
rushed him off with orders. He noticed the passage of shot and shell
with absolute indifference. That he actually sang, "Old Joe Hooker,
get out of the Wilderness," I vouch for. It was veritably his slogan at
Chancellorsville.

The Confederates were greatly outnumbered, and we were fighting more than twice as many, and attacking in the open, while the
Yankees had protective breastworks.

To Lee and Jackson no doubt are due the strategic thoughts that
outgeneraled Hooker and his mighty army, but to General Stuart is

due the energetic following out of their plans. He handled the infantry at Chancellorsville quite as well as he handled the cavalry, and for this it appears he has never received the great credit due him. He filled Jackson's shoes there at Jackson's special request, and doubtless he filled the immortal Jackson's place as no one else could have done.

5

Brandy Station

After the Battle of Chancellorsville, which the Confederates considered a great victory, the strength of the Army of Northern Virginia, reinforced by the return of Longstreet's Corps, was greater than ever before. The army was proud of itself. The commanding general and every man under him firmly believed that it was invincible. The men, indeed, seemed eager to fight again and get it over with. The Army did not realize that, though Hooker's losses were in fact somewhat greater than theirs, proportionately they were less, and the North had many more men to draw from. It did not occur to the Southerners that the Army of the Potomac even under a new commander could yet prove formidable.

The cavalry division of J. E. B. Stuart had some rest that May, and Frank Robertson was able to get home to Richmond for a week. He then wrote to his father on May 22, 1863, from the cavalry's camp near Culpeper Court House:

> I have only time before dark to drop you a hasty note. I reached here safely Wednesday evening, being ignorant of the change of HeadQuarters until I got to Orange C.H. We are now camped about half a mile from the town on a high shady hill with a good spring and excellent pasturage near at hand and in every respect bettered by the change. My horses I found much improved by their weeks rest, but still thin and surely in need of Sam's attention.[1]
>
> The grand Cavalry Review took place this morning [at Brandy Station] and was one of the most imposing scenes I ever witnessed. First and at the head of the column, came the Artillery, twelve guns strong, and immediately behind, the Cavalry in Column of squad-

rons—Gen. Hampton's Brigade in advance—Gen. [W. H. F. "Rooney"]
Lee's next and Gen. Fitz Lee's bringing up the rear,—about five thousand men in all and generally well mounted.

After passing thus before the General and Staff at a slow gait,
the Artillery drew up in line of battle on an opposite hill where they
remained until the head of the Column again approached our position, when they unlimbered and commenced a heavy cannonade—
the Cavalry Division at the same time moving up at a brisk trot and
each Squadron as it reached a certain spot, charging with a yell that
almost drowned the roar of the opposite batteries,—the rush of such
large bodies of men amid the booming of cannon and clashing of sabres produced a very pleasant excitement and somehow inspired me
with a confidence in our cause and an assurance of eventual success
difficult to account for, now that it is all over.

Gen. [George W.] Randolph and Maj. Peyton came up from Richmond to witness it, and I am very sorry that I did not know certainly
when it was going to take place until too late to let you know in time
to get here.[2]

If Sam is only slightly indisposed I think it probable he would
recover here as soon as in Richmond and if we made an advance movement before he was well, he might remain with the wagons, but do
just as you think best. If he comes, don't forget to send my jacket and
pants by him or by any other opportunity you may have, also my hat.

It is so dark I can't see to write any more. We have no candles. I
have gotten almost well again, but suffer a good deal with headaches.

Writing again on May 24, the young engineer sought his sister
Kate's help with some problems he was facing:

As we may be here for several weeks yet and I hear the fishing is
very good in the vicinity, I write to ask you to get me some fishing
tackle and send it either by Sam or in a letter. I want two lines without corks and about twelve or fifteen hooks of different sizes, not much
smaller than this [drawing of small fishhook appears here] or larger
than this [drawing of larger fishhook appears here]. I write for so
many because several of the staff have requested me to get enough
for them also. Wyndham will get them for you.

If my jacket is still unfinished I should like the arms to be trimed
[sic] with buff & gold lace.[3] I directed otherwise, but the staff have
all fixed up to such an alarming extent that I shall have to follow
suit, or be taken for a courier. Cousin William will have it done if you
will get Wyndham to tell him. I want a cord of buff [drawing of jacket
sleeve appears here] run around the sleeve marking the edge of the
cuffs if there were any.

Please get me a piece of sponge. I was about to say as large as
your hand, but considering it a matter of serious doubt whether a

common hat could contain both that & my head, a piece half the size will do.

I am going down to Germana [Germanna] to day to get my clothes & also for another purpose which I will tell you of, one of these days perhaps.

I am almost well again, but still in a bad humor—about what I can't imagine. I will write a larger letter when I return.

Robertson's concerns over fish and uniforms were soon overshadowed by more important events. In a letter to his father dated May 30 he wrote of an assignment he had just been given: "Mr. B. [Capt. W. W. Blackford], Tom Price and myself received orders today to make a topographical survey of the North bank of the Rappahannock, extending from the Rail Road to the mouth of the Rapidan—as it is fifteen to twenty miles between, we will probably be absent several days."

Whether the three engineers ever completed their survey is unknown. Certainly other matters required their attention as well.

By the end of May the brigades of William E. "Grumble" Jones and of Beverly H. Robertson[4] had rejoined the cavalry division, which was further strengthened by the return of men who had been absent on sick leave or in quest of fresh horses, as well as by a few recruits. The division was bigger than it had ever been before numbering almost ten thousand. Ten thousand men under the command of a young officer who hardly two years earlier had never commanded a hundred! Stuart could quite justify himself in ordering a second grand cavalry review for all 9,536 men on June 5—not that he was averse to doing so. He invited General Lee to the pageant and his officers invited every pretty girl for miles around, including some from Richmond and Charlottesville.

The night before the review, a dance was given in the Court House, and another the night following. The enthusiasm of the men in the ranks for this gallivanting is not recorded, but it was a gala time for the bachelor officers and for the young ladies, who loved it all. The first review had been magnificent but with twice as many mounted men and twenty-four guns, the one on June 5 was awe-inspiring. The only trouble was that the commanding general was so immersed in his plans for the invasion of the North that he could not get there.

General Lee, however, did consider it important for him personally to inspect the cavalry division, so he suggested another review on the 8th. Stuart rejoiced to concur with his wishes, though it is not likely that many of his troopers shared in his joy. On the

7th he had moved his headquarters five miles northeast of his former camp near Culpeper to Fleetwood Hill, overlooking the plain of Brandy Station, in preparation for his third grand cavalry review. Major H. B. McClellan,[5] formerly adjutant of the 3rd Virginia Cavalry, who had succeeded Norman R. FitzHugh[6] as adjutant on Stuart's staff, wrote of this review, "Much less display was attempted on this occasion, for General Lee, always careful not to tax his men unnecessarily, would not allow the cavalry to take the gallop, nor would he permit the artillerymen to work their guns. He would reserve all their strength for the serious work which must shortly ensue."[7]

Captain Robertson wrote of the review in 1926:

> Von Borcke formed the staff in line and as the head of the cavalry column approached, squadron front, our staff rode out in front in single line. Just before passing General Lee and the spectators, General Stuart ordered me to go to a hill where General W. E. Jones' brigade looked scattered around generally as if unknowing of the Grand Review, and "ask him why his command was not ready for review." I located General Jones by knowing his claybank horse. He was lying on the ground and apparently oblivious of everything that was going on. I delivered my message. He blazed all sorts of language at me, and I rode from under with no answer for a return message. I noted, however, his bugles blew "boots and saddles," and his brigade was promptly on the move.

Bitter hatred of long standing existed between Brig. Gen. William E. Jones and Maj. Gen. J. E. B. Stuart. Jones had graduated from West Point two years before Stuart entered the Academy. He resigned his commission as lieutenant of cavalry in 1857 and spent the next four years farming near Abingdon. When Virginia seceded, he began his career in the Confederate Army as a captain. Stuart, on the other hand, in May 1861, gave up his commission as captain of cavalry in the United States Army to fight for Virginia. He was at once appointed lieutenant colonel of infantry in the army of his state. A few weeks later he was colonel of cavalry in the Confederate States Army, and Captain Jones had a company in his regiment, the 1st Virginia. Stuart became a brigadier general on September 24, 1861, and a major general on July 25, 1862. Jones was made a brigadier, contrary to Stuart's wishes, in the fall of 1862, the last promotion he ever received. Perhaps the disparity in rank in the new army was in part responsible for the enmity between Jones and Stuart. It is likely that "Grumble Jones" recognized Stuart's messenger as an Abingdon boy just as Frank recog-

nized the General's claybank horse, and it is understandable that
he did not like to receive a message of reproof delivered by a strip-
ling from his home town. Robertson continued:

> I never changed or modified General Stuart's messages. Several
> times I received violent language in return,—I was a sort of cushion,
> as it were, between the two generals in communication. Some of the
> generals could be very rude to us boy riders of the staff. I nursed
> resentment towards them and am still doing so, but all of those old
> boys died off before I could demand apologies. Some, or perhaps most
> of them, were kindly and gentle to all; notable in this way, as my
> experience went, were General Lee himself, General Stonewall Jack-
> son, General [William Dorsey] Pender, General [John B.] Gordon,
> General Terry, General Joe Johnston, General [James] Dearing and
> General Wade Hampton.[8]

> Our grand cavalry review was voted a great success, but many a
> fine young fellow was next day resting in a soldier's grave.

This third cavalry review undoubtedly was a great success.
General Lee, in an oft-quoted letter to his wife that evening remarked, "Stuart was in all his glory," and certainly nobody enjoyed
the day more than he.

The following morning Lt. Gen. Richard S. Ewell was to start
for Pennsylvania, soon to be followed by Longstreet and Hill. Stuart
was instructed to cross the Rappahannock and cover their right
flank on the march. After the grand review the cavalrymen walked
their horses to their bivouac areas to complete their preparations
for an early start on June 9. Fitz Lee's Brigade[9] with a battery of
horse artillery—Captain James Breathed's[10]—marched five miles
northwest of Fleetwood Hill, beyond the Hazel River. All the other
brigades were located south of this little river or on the
Rappahannock. Just east of the northwest end of Fleetwood Hill
was Rooney Lee's Brigade, with pickets at Welford's Ford across
the Hazel, about two miles west of where that river flows into the
larger one. In the woods around St. James Church was Grumble
Jones, who had placed strong pickets at Beverly Ford across the
Rappahannock, a mile above the railroad bridge. South of Jones's
Brigade was Hampton's, extending four miles down to Stevensburg.
East of these was Beverly Robertson's small brigade. Robertson
posted a picket at Kelly's Ford, four miles downstream from the
railroad bridge. Stuart and his staff spent the night under two
tent flies on Fleetwood Hill.

St. James Church was about a mile in front of the center of
Fleetwood Hill, a little more than two miles from Welford's Ford

Lt. Gen. John Brown Gordon of Georgia. A civilian before the war, Gordon became one of Lee's best fighting generals and closest confidants by the close of the conflict.

and Beverly Ford to the north, and a scant two miles from Brandy Station to the southeast. All of the horse artillery, except that with Fitz Lee, was between the two upper fords and the church, which was in the center of things. Kelly's Ford was five miles in a straight line to the east of the church, a little more by the north road, considerably more by the south road.

These dispositions were made in the belief that all was quiet on the other side of the Rappahannock, as indeed it appeared to be at dusk. Not a single campfire was to be seen beyond the river that night. The Confederates did not know that the enemy suspected something was afoot south of the river and that General Alfred Pleasonton, after almost a year of combat, was learning from an excellent teacher how to fight cavalry. Nor did the Rebels know that the Yankees had some brilliant young leaders who were coming fast: John Buford[11] (who rather belonged to Pleasonton's generation), David Gregg,[12] Judson Kilpatrick,[13] and Alfred Duffie.[14] All of them would be heard from again.

The Rebels made the acquaintance of Pleasonton and his young commanders quite early on the morning of June 9. What followed was the greatest cavalry battle on the North American continent. On June 12, 1863, Robertson wrote to his sister and told her of the battle:

> It gives me pleasure to write you that once more I have passed thro' the thickest of the fight unscathed. We were waked on the morn-

ing of the 9th by the rattling fire of our pickets as they slowly fell back before the heavy masses of Cavalry which the enemy were throwing across the river at Beverly's Ford. Of course everything and everybody were immediately on the stir. The wagon trains were in motion first and went thundering to the rear mid clouds of dust— then came the cavalry regiments at a trot with here and there a battery of artillery,—all hurrying to the front with the greatest speed possible.

As it was some time before the Gen. Commanding changed his base, I had ample opportunity to witness all the preparatory arrangements, both offensive and defensive, for the coming fight. With the aid of Mr. [Capt. W. W.] Blackford's glass, I saw distinctly the advance of the Yankee skirmishers and the heavy line of battle following closely in their rear—they advanced cautiously but boldly until within range of our batteries and the advanced skirmishers of the supporting Regiments and squadron after squadron dashed to the front until it began to sound a little like Chancellorsville.

About this time Gen. Stuart ordered me to Brandy Station to take charge of the dismounted men of Hampton's Brigade and post them on the road leading from that point to Kelly's Ford, as he anticipated what afterwards took place, that the enemy would cross at that ford and endeavor to get in our rear. On getting to Brandy, I found Capt. [Theodore G.] Barker (Hampton's Adjutant Gen.) who informed me that there were no dismounted men belonging to Hampton's Brigade on the field and I at once galloped back and reported to Gen. Stuart, who I found far to the front, immediately in rear of the skirmishers.[15] As he seems to consider me particularly suitable to manage foot soldiers, and left me to form them in line and advance through the woods until the enemy was found, which after much difficulty I succeeded in doing.

Brig. Gen. David McMurtrie Gregg was one of the Union cavalry's rising stars in June 1863.

When I next found the General he was near the old brick church in the woods. He was behind one of our batteries which was playing on a column of Yankee Infantry [Brig. Gen. Adelbert Ames' men] advancing from the river [at Beverly Ford] to support their Skirmishers who were falling back before Gen. Rooney Lee's brigade at our extreme left. We had been there I suppose 15 or 20 minutes when a courier dashed up and reported the enemy at Brandy Station, immediately in our rear and advancing rapidly upon the hill where we had been camped and which commanded the surrounding country for miles.

For the first time the Gen. looked excited and ordered me to go to Gen. Hampton as fast as a horse could go and tell him to send back to this hill a regiment at a gallop. Away I went over ditches, fences, mire and everything else at a breakneck neck speed for about a mile, delivered my orders, started the Regiment and returned nearly as fast with a message from General Hampton, but on reaching the place where I had left the General he was gone as also most of the cannon—the latter I could see dashing across the field at a gallop to get possession of the hill before the Yankees. From where I was I could see the most exciting scene I ever witnessed—on one side of the high hill were dense columns of Yankee Cavalry galloping up in beautiful order and on the other side our ragged troopers, one or two regiments in good order, but the rest one confused mass of flying horsemen and both sides straining every nerve and muscle to reach the hill first. The enemy however had the advantage and while one of their batteries made for the hill, another unlimbered on a slight elevation opposite and opened fire on a few of our men who had been on the hill all the while with our adjutant General (Maj. McClelland [H.B. McClellan]).[16]

I was considerably puzzled to know where to go or what to do, but concluded the General must be making for the hill with the rest, I galloped on, but on getting nearly to the top met a large body of Yankees who were sweeping everything before them. [Lieutenant Chiswell] Dabney[17] (who was with me), as soon as we had recovered from our precipitate retreat, told me that the General was on the right and we rode in that direction and reached the top of the hill several hundred yards further on. When we reached the top we saw a regiment or two of our men, who had charged around the left of the hill, pursuing a large body of Yankees who were flying towards Brandy Station. I supposed at once that the hill was in our possession, on seeing our men were on the opposite side and put up my pistol and rode very composedly right into the head of the eighth Illinois who came charging and yelling around a skirt of trees, right on the heels of the twelfth Virginia Cavalry, who had taken to the most inglorious flight.

(Left) Brig. Gen. Hugh Judson Kilpatrick earned the name "Kilcavalry" because of the manner in which he pushed the men and horses under his command. However, his aggressive style helped to give the Federal mounted arm the confidence it needed to stand up to Stuart's troopers.

(Right) Brig. Gen. Alfred Napoleon Alexander Duffié had followed orders at Brandy Station and missed a chance to be the hero of the hour. In mid-June 1863 his First Rhode Island Cavalry was sacrificed in a hopeless expedition behind Confederate lines.

    With my usual good luck I was obliged to run once more for my life, with a Yankee orderly Sergeant right at my heels popping away at my back every jump of his horse—how he happened to miss me I can't imagine, for a fairer mark or a more helpless one was never presented. I was riding Bostona and do what I could, I could neither turn her to the right or left—nor could I draw my pistol, every time I attempted to unbutton the pistol holster, she commenced blundering, absolutely it seemed on purpose, and I was forced to withdraw my hand to grasp the rein and hold her up—for at least two hundred yards this race kept up and I could see the fellow raise his pistol between his horse's ears and take deliberate aim, but fortunately I was not even grazed, though one of the balls cut a slight furrow in Bostona's leg.

Von Borcke and Dabney were both in the route [sic], but some distance ahead of me. Bostona is so awkward and difficult to turn, that when the General gives me an order to the rear and I endeavor to turn she generally manages to sweep the road clear of both staff and couriers and always produces a laugh—if I want to turn to the left, I grasp the left rein firmly and pull her head in that direction at the same time extending my left foot as far to the rear as possible and spurring most furiously—I find that the only way of accomplishing the left about wheel.

When I again joined the General the hill had been cleared of the Yankees and we had captured the battery which they had endeavored to place on top of it. The fight was still raging on the left and Gen. [Rooney] Lee had been forced to fall back. I was again in the thickest of the fight and had nearly got to Gen. Lee with orders when he was wounded. At another time a percussion shell struck the ground about ten yards beyond a group of us who were lying in the shade of a cherry tree, and bounded right into the midst of us, stopping within a yard and a half of my head, but fortunately not exploding. I could write a great deal more about the fight but am quite tired and sleepy and you must wait till another time. Mr. [Capt. W. W.] Blackford was sent down to Gen. R. E. Lee at Culpeper and I did not see much of him during the fight, though he saw the most glorious thing of the day, the retaking of the hill by Col. [P. M. B.] Young[18] of Cobb's Legion while I was skedaddling with the routed twelfth.

The fight lasted from sunrise to sunset and is by far the greatest Cavalry fight of the War. Our loss was about 400, killed, wounded and missing. The Yankees about 700 and three pieces of artillery.[19] Capt. Fairleigh [William D. Farley][20] (Vol. Aide) was killed, Capt. [Benjamin S.] White[21] also one of the General staff was shot through the ear and neck and Lieut. [Robert H.] Goldsborough[22] (regular Aide) is missing, supposed to be a prisoner, who with Pelham, Hullion [Walter Q. Hullihen], and [Channing] Price make a very heavy loss of a General in three months.

I think we will probably move in a day or two, I don't know certainly, but it is generally believed, across the Rappahannock. I suppose ere this you are all at the Meadows—how I would like to pay you a short visit up there, but unless I am wounded, I suppose there is little chance this summer.

Enclosed I send you a piece of silk from one of the Yankee flags we captured. I have also the brass spear head of a flag staff but it is too heavy to enclose. Tell Aunt Charlott Gilbert [her grandson] is well and he and Sam are both riged [sic] out in Yankee clothes,

In 1926, he supplied further vivid details as to what happened that summer morning on Fleetwood Hill:

> At daybreak, June 9th, our camp on Fleetwood Hill was roused by picket firing on the Rappahannock, a mile or so east. I remember Captain William D. Farley threw his hat in the air and yelled, "Hurrah, we're going to have a fight!" His exuberance was cooled in death that evening.
>
> Our cavalry was soon in motion covering the Yankee advance. My first order was to collect all the dismounted men with the wagon train at Brandy Station, march them down the Kelly Ford road, picket and watch the same. I found all the dismounts had gone with the wagon train, and I immediately reported this to the General. It seemed to worry him, for as it proved afterwards, he anticipated a possible advance of the enemy by this Ford.
>
> General Stuart was near an old church in the woods watching the rather slack of the Yanks to advance from the river, when Frank [H.] Deane (an old school mate of mine and a courier attached to Stuart's headquarters) dashed up full speed through the woods, crying as he came,
>
> "General, the Yankees are at Brandy Station!"
>
> This meant they were exactly in our rear, and for the first and only time while I was with him the general was much excited.
>
> He called out "Where's my staff?" and I replied, "Here."
>
> "Go, go fast to General Hampton, and tell him to send a regiment at a gallop!"
>
> I didn't know where General Hampton was, but he pointed and I went that way. I saw a group of cavalry across a deep ditch. They seemed also excited and, as I rode along the ditch looking for a crossing, a man dashed off from this group to meet me. He was one of Hampton's staff and I delivered my orders and paused a moment to see the regiment go to the rear at a gallop.[23]
>
> General Hampton was over half a mile from the church mentioned, and I am sure that it was not more than ten minutes before that regiment was at a gallop to stay that rear attack. All things considered, it was the speediest all around movement I ever remember, and one that doubtless saved us a great disaster. Some outrageous negligence allowed [Brig. Gen. David M. Gregg's] great cavalry column to cross at Kelly's Ford and advance unhindered upon the rear of Stuart's Cavalry on the firing line, and I've always wondered that nothing was ever done about it.

The young engineer was not alone in thinking that General Beverly Robertson had bungled that day, but he had only two regiments, perhaps not 500 men, and Gregg had five times that number. General Robertson had moved to strong ground on the north side of the road from Kelly's Ford to Brandy and, dug in about two miles from the ford, was between it and the railroad bridge. He had sent word to Stuart that the enemy had crossed the river, and he considered he was obeying orders by holding his ground. But Gregg chose the more circuitous south road to Brandy Station, and this he had all to himself. Yet Robertson's "command...was not at any time actively engaged,"[24] so he had not a single casualty to report.

Luck, however, did not entirely forsake Stuart that day. Pleasonton had planned for Buford to cross the Rappahannock before dawn, while Gregg was fording it about five and half miles downstream. They were to meet at Brandy, completing a pincers movement on the Confederate cavalry. Duffie, though, was three hours late getting to Kelly's Ford, and Gregg, for reasons he never gave, decided to wait for him. It was then nearly 6 o'clock, three hours after the scheduled hour, that Gregg began to cross the river. If the plan had been carried out as Pleasonton originally ordered, the usefulness of the cavalry of the Army of Northern Virginia (if not the whole cavalry division itself) might have been destroyed that day.

The memoir continues:

> I spent a full hour looking for my General. When I reached Fleetwood Hill, our headquarters tents had disappeared. One of our horse artillery batteries was firing upon a long line of Yanks coming rapidly towards the hill.[25] [These were the men who had crossed at Kelly's Ford.] Frank Deane's cry was the first intimation General Stuart had that the Yanks had crossed at this ford.[26]
>
> Besides Hampton's regiment[27] others were riding hard to meet this unexpected attack.[28] The battle was now on in earnest. Fleetwood Hill was captured and recaptured several times, as was one of the batteries on its slope. This was all horseback and sabre combat and would have been enjoyable had I been in an airplane.[29] There was a general mix-up battle—indeed there was no line. Every regiment seemed to be doing its fighting regardless of other regiments.
>
> Still trying to locate General Stuart, I rode through a strip of pines and emerged directly in front of a charging regiment of Yanks in hot pursuit of a part of the 12th Virginia Cavalry. Major von Borcke and Captain [Benjamin S.] White I saw speeding in front of me,—the latter was shot through the neck; his neck seemed limber and useful in watching the rear, but an hour or so afterwards it seemed very stiff and useless. I joked him about it frequently. The 11th Virginia [Col. Lunsford L. Lomax][30] charged in turn those charging Yanks and cap-

tured a big slice of them. This no doubt saved old Von, White and myself from capture, as a high fence rose across our line of retreat, and I was riding Bostona, not Miranda, that day.

Bostona was a thoroughbred raised by my father. She was long and tall and harder to turn around than a six-horse wagon, and it required a half a mile to get her fully under way. So, when I rode out of the pine thicket not twenty-five yards in front of the charging Yanks, I had slight hope of escaping. I believe that, but for the 11th Virginia, I would have landed in a Yankee prison. Bostona was a good-meaning, poor raw-boned creature, and I swapped her afterwards for a large mare I somehow found tied in the woods of Pennsylvania.

When the 9th Virginia first charged up the hill, General [Rooney] Lee was upon its left flank, encouraging the men of his old regiment. Just before he reached the crest of the hill, he was severely wounded. I was carrying a message to General Rooney Lee from General Stuart and was within a few yards of him when he was wounded. I little thought then that I should afterwards become one of his staff. There was some hitch as to who was next in command, and I made much riding to do between General Stuart and Colonels [John R.] Chambliss[31] and [James L.] Davis[32] of the 13th and 10th Virginia Regiments respectively ere this was settled [in favor of Colonel Chambliss]. I saw Davis killed in the streets of Hagerstown afterwards. Chambliss was also later killed [at Black Bottom, August 16, 1864].

The result of all this confused battling was the driving back of the Yanks across the Rappahannock River, though it was an all day fight and, as usual, we were greatly outnumbered.[33] One result of incalculable importance certainly did follow this battle,—it made the Federal cavalry. Up to that time confessedly inferior to the Southern horsemen, they gained on this day that confidence in themselves and in their commanders which enabled them to contest so fiercely the subsequent battlefields of June, July and October. Returning from the front late that day with Captain Blackford, we came across a beautiful sorrel horse standing with his foreleg off at the knee. Thinking to put him out of his misery, I rode up some eight feet in front of him and fired at the spot on his forehead. At the crack of the pistol, he sprang forward, knocking my horse down, bruising my leg and covering me with blood which gushed from his mouth. All hands thought I was wounded when I reached camp and went limping about in my bloody clothes.

By evening we were hungry and any sort of food was acceptable. Towards the close of this battle, the General stopped under a big cherry tree and told his young staff to seek rations and to pitch him down a few. Several of us were up the tree in

Brig. Gen. John Randolph Chambliss assumed command of "Rooney" Lee's brigade after that officer was wounded at Brandy Station.

a moment,—a shell passed through the tree and the limb and the young staff officers descended together. The General was highly diverted, and he cried out, "What's the matter, boys? Cherries getting sour?"

General Stuart's high spirits seemed unquenchable and he had a wonderful sense of humor always. A day or two before we had raided a tree in a front yard and were enjoying the cherries when an old lady appeared suddenly around the house with a long pole in her hands. She silently but effectively went into action with that pole. As Captain [William D.] Farley hit the ground, the pole hit him. The General yelled, "Biggs, blow the retreat!" Which Biggs did at once. Farley was our telegraph expert: he would climb poles within the Yankee lines and corral some of their secret messages with a small machine he carried. He also was armed with a long range rifle that used an explosive shell; he used this weapon to blow up artillery caissons and ammunition wagons.

Our camp being re-established on Fleetwood Hill, we slept that night the sleep of the exhausted; lying all around us were many Rebs and Yanks who slept the sleep that has no waking. Next day I made Sam, my valet-de-chambre, strip a dead Yankee and rehabilitate himself in a fancy new Yank uniform. He was badly in need of a change. The General didn't know Sam, and asked him what command he belonged to. Sam was much embarrassed, but replied, "I belongs to Marse Frank." Which greatly amused the onlookers...

Riding among the cedars around our camp I found the polished head of a Yankee guidon staff sticking in one of the trees. It was a pretty souvenir of the battle, and now that I have girls of my own,

I regret that I gave it to one in Richmond. I acquired here too a new Colt pistol, which is still with me. My old pistol was too small, and my delight was great when I hung this prize on my belt.

We missed our departed comrades.

A few days before Brandy Station Stuart had sent home the one Richmond reporter in his camp. After the battle, the capital papers had to draw their accounts of the engagement from Northern journals, all of which played it up as a great Federal victory. This it was not, but after the pomp of the grand cavalry reviews it must have been galling to the General to read in the papers "the sarcastic talk of an exposed rear and of surprise."

Even Captain William Blackford's brother Charles, of Longstreet's staff (Charles did not share his older brother's admiration of Stuart), wrote to his wife on June 12: "The cavalry fight at Brandy Station can hardly be called a victory. Stuart was certainly surprised and but for the supreme gallantry of his subordinate officers and the men of his command, it would have been a day of disaster and disgrace.... Stuart is blamed very much, but whether fairly or not I am not sufficiently well informed to say."[34]

In truth, Stuart held the field and could rightfully claim the victory. His junior officers and their men did indeed fight hard, but Stuart deserved credit for keeping his head, holding the enemy at St. James Church, and turning on Gregg in time to win the day—and this without the help of Robertson who was supposed to be guarding the flank around which Gregg came. In the end, Robert E. Lee was not displeased with his cavalry chief regardless of what the Richmond papers had to say.

6

The Gettysburg Campaign

By the late spring of 1863 Lee's men and horses were slowly starving. Northern Virginia, never blessed with a very fertile soil, by then had been stripped bare. Lee had no choice but to look for food and fodder in the North. By June 17, Ewell, with the Second Corps, originally Jackson's and for one glorious day at Chancellorsville, Stuart's, had handily taken Winchester and was beginning to ford the Potomac. Longstreet, two days out from Culpeper, was climbing the Blue Ridge on his way into the Valley. Pleasonton was still trying to find out what the Rebels were up to. It was Stuart's job to see that he did not succeed. In the vicinity of Aldie, with the sabres of Buford and Gregg, Pleasonton was making things lively for Fitz Lee's Brigade, still under the command of Col. Thomas T. Munford. Robertson continues his narrative:

> I do not remember just where we went from Fleetwood. I shall simply continue this ramshackled narrative as I recall the salient points of my personal experiences. We were again in Middleburg [June 17], only General Stuart and staff; Munford's brigade had preceded us, and six or eight miles behind was following Robertson's brigade. We were in the yard of a house that had been burned, eating our scanty mid-day ration. A courier dashed up at full speed to say, "A regiment of Yankees are coming into town at a trot." Away went our outfit due west towards [General] Robertson's approaching command. About a half a mile out, the General suddenly pulled up and called "Robertson." I rode to the front. I think he probably selected me knowing the speed and endurance of Miranda.

Aldie, Middleburg, and Upperville, the scene of desperate cavalry fighting from June 17 to 21.

"Go back," he said, "go tell Munford the enemy are behind him, and to press a guide,[1] and join me by roundabout roads at Rector's Cross Roads tonight. You will find him at Aldie." Aldie was about six miles from Middleburg. "Quick," he added, "and look out for yourself, Robertson."

"Goodbye, Robertson," was the cheering send off from my comrades and it meant more than usual, for wasn't I riding right into a full regiment of Yankee cavalry? Back I went and down Middleburg's deserted street (except for one young lady with a frightened face upon a porch, not a soul was visible), I rode full speed, as all depended upon my passing through before the Yankees entered. As I crossed the street leading south, it seemed full of Yankees, some only forty yards away. Then we had it. Yells and cuss words greeted my ears, and leaden messengers passed me by or kicked up dust around the flying feet of my incomparable little mare. For three miles or more the chase continued, but the gap between us widened. Only one blaze-faced sorrel could hold Miranda's speed, his rider occasionally sending me a bullet. I did not respond until going up a long hill when suddenly I pulled up and shot in return. This stopped the race. I saw Blaze Face turn as I fired and his rider seemed loose in the saddle. I didn't have time to go back to inquire after his health, nor did I cease to gallop until my message was delivered to Colonel Munford.

I found Fitz Lee's brigade (Munford of the 2nd Virginia Cavalry at the time, was commanding the brigade in the absence of General Lee, still laid up) engaged in a lively fight which was becoming quite warm. Munford called it off as soon as he received my message, pressed a guide and we joined General Stuart that night.

Col. Thomas Taylor Munford led Fitz Lee's Brigade at Brandy Station when that officer was unable to command because of illness.

Colonel Alfred Duffie had come through Thoroughfare Gap early that morning with the 1st Rhode Island Cavalry, to serve as the left flank of Gregg's Brigade. They were ordered to spend the night of the 17th in Middleburg. This little town lies on the west slope of Bull Run Mountain, on the pike from Aldie, six miles to the East. The turnpike goes on west twelve miles to Upperville, which stands guard at the eastern approach to Ashby's Gap through the Blue Ridge. In this gap nestles the village of Paris; a few miles beyond, Winchester dominates the lower (or northeastern) end of the Valley of Virginia. Duffie drove Stuart out of Middleburg, but Stuart soon returned with Robertson's Brigade, and threw the Rhode Islanders they did not kill or capture back into the open arms of Chambliss' Brigade, approaching Middleburg from the south. The next day Duffie believed that he had lost all but 32 of his 300 officers and men. About seventy more drifted in and a month later he had recruited his regiment again up to 300.[2]

General Stuart did not, however, have long to enjoy the hospitality of Middleburg, because of General Pleasonton's persistent efforts to break through his screen in order to find out what the Confederate Army was doing in the Valley. Stuart did not enjoy the defensive role thus thrust upon him. Moreover, he learned from a captured dispatch that three brigades of Northern infantry were supporting the numerically superior enemy cavalry. He had to ask for reinforcement from Longstreet who supplied the infantry. But neither the grey nor the blue cavalry knew of their presence.

The engagement which followed was remembered by Robertson in his memoirs:

> Next day the enemy advanced in force, cavalry backed by infantry. We were forced back from Middleburg to Upperville, and thence to Paris in the Blue Ridge. Cavalry backed by infantry prove a tough proposition to cavalry alone. The cavalry may be routed and driven back to the infantry,—but the latter know they can't run away from cavalry and find it safer to stand and fight.
>
> Major von Borcke was badly wounded in the neck. He kindly mentions me as having figured in getting him off the field. I was sitting on my horse right by him and heard the bullet strike. The impact was so loud that I thought a fragment of shell had struck a fence near us,—but then I saw Von reel in his saddle, and I jumped from my horse just in time to ease him down with Captain Blackford's help. As we were being driven back at the time,— with infantry backing up their cavalry while we had none—it was difficult indeed to get von Borcke off the field and save him from capture; I went back for

an ambulance and helped drag him into it. I saw the cut in his neck, and, thinking it only a graze wound, told him so. He said, "Oh, I hurt to death'." I then saw blood on his lips. The ball had entered the neck and gone down into his lungs. He was sent to Richmond, and when I next saw him [in December 1864] he had lost 80 pounds, he told me. (He asked me to take his farewell dinner with him at the Spotswood Hotel, and the next day he left to run the blockade from Wilmington, N. C. to his home in Germany. He was "a free lance," on the weaker side, and he proved a brave and valiant soldier. He afterwards held high rank in the Franco-Prussian War.)[3]

The Yankees saw that an important member of Stuart's headquarters had been badly hurt, and they thought for a time that it was General Stuart himself. They were intent on capturing this wounded officer, and it was not a simple matter to hide von Borcke's 240 pounds. The ambulance took him rapidly into Upperville, he threatening to shoot the driver in the back if he didn't slow down, to the home of Dr. Talcott Eliason, where under happier circumstances he had been a guest a number of times. He was put to bed in the parlor and everything possible done to make him comfortable. The doctor's blind ten-year-old daughter, a great pet of Von's, wept bitterly. Eliason did not think the giant Prussian could live through the night and, in accordance with the custom of the day, told him so. In the course of the afternoon he had many visitors including General Stuart himself, who, according to von Borcke, was much moved.[4]

Maj. Johann August Heinrich Heros von Borcke, Stuart's assistant adjutant and inspector general, was severely wounded on June 19, 1863, at the Battle of Middleburg.

The next day there was heavy fighting around Upperville. The morning of the 21st General Stuart came by Dr. Eliason's house again. He admitted to von Borcke that he might be driven back, but, if so, he promised to send an ambulance to save him from the oncoming Yankees. Both realized that the wounded man should not be moved if it could be helped. Soon von Borcke's old Prussian friend, Captain Justus Scheibert,[5] serving on Longstreet's staff, arrived with Longstreet's personal ambulance, but Von declined to go with him. When a messenger from Stuart came to announce that the fall of Upperville was imminent, he did consent to being moved to a farmhouse a couple of miles away. Later in the day a Federal search party spent half an hour at the farm looking for him. "I resolved, with desperate energy," the Major reported later, "not to die without resistance. I reached down my arm with a painful effort, and placing my unsheathed sword, and my revolver already cocked, on the bed, prepared to shoot down the first of the enemy's troopers who should enter."[6] None of the Yankee troopers did succeed in finding him.

Lieutenant Robertson's friend and hero had to be left behind as the cavalry moved on. There was scant hope for his life, but to everyone's surprise, he rallied amazingly, and in a few days he was "allowed to sit up an hour or two in the verandah to enjoy the cool aromatic breeze traveling hither from the beautiful Blue Ridge Mountains."[7] After a few weeks, "the frequency of Federal scouting parties crossing the Potomac rendered it dangerous that he should remain,"[8] so he left for Richmond, where he was welcomed by the father of Channing and Tom Price into his home. In the heat of the Richmond summer he went down hill, so toward the end of August he sought refuge with friends in Hanover. For two long months he wasted away, and his life was despaired of. The first day he got up he was "startled by a report that a body of Federals were approaching the house; and, dreading the danger of capture more than the consequences of exposure,"[9] he fled back to the home of the Prices in Richmond, where he was again confined to bed for a couple of months.

In January 1864, he was afforded great satisfaction by "a joint resolution of thanks by both Houses of the Confederate Congress. Lafayette was the last foreigner to whom this honor was accorded in America, and out of courtesy the resolution was couched in the same words as had been used on that occasion, and which were as follows:

> Whereas Maj. Heros von Borcke, of Prussia, assistant adjutant and inspector general of the cavalry corps of the Army of Northern Virginia, having left his own country to assist in securing the independence of ours, and by his personal gallantry in the field having won the admiration of his comrades as well as that of the commanding general, all of whom deeply sympathize with him in his present suffering from wounds received in battle:
>
> Therefore:
>
> Resolved by the Congress of the Confederate States of America. That the thanks of the Congress are due, and the same are hereby tendered, to Major Heros von Borcke, for his self-sacrificing devotion to our Confederacy, and for his distinguished service in support of its cause.
>
> Resolved, That a copy of the foregoing resolution be transmitted to Major von Borcke by the President of the Confederate States.

Von Borcke wrote in response to the honor: "This document[10] I received with a very flattering autograph letter from the President, which was followed by hundreds of congratulatory epistles from my comrades in the army, and from friends in all parts of the country."[11]

Von's charm and social graces made him a great favorite in Richmond society that winter, and he enjoyed the attentions showered upon him. If he realized that his spectacular military career enhanced his prestige in the eyes of the Confederate belles, he enjoyed it the more. One of the most prominent of these young ladies, Miss Constance Cary, forty years later in describing the special life of Richmond that last awful year, mentioned him several times.

Von Borcke saw Stuart whenever he came to the capital, and twice he was royally welcomed to his camp near Culpeper. With the return of spring, he felt stronger and repeatedly he tried to take the field again, but each time he was thrown back to bed, so he had to be content himself with a desk job in Richmond. On May 11, 1864, however, the sound of the horse artillery guns so near being too much for him, Major von Borcke commandeered a horse and tried to join his chief. Though these exertions brought on another severe hemorrhage, when Dr. [Charles] Brewer told him next morning that Stuart, grievously wounded, was asking for him, Von hastened to his bedside.

In the summer of 1864 General George Wythe Randolph had recommended that von Borcke be made a brigadier general and placed in command of all cavalry in the vicinity of Richmond for the protection of the city. General Lee approved of this plan: "Ma-

jor von Borcke is an officer of singular worth and merit, of great
seal and gallantry, and merits every consideration." But the War
Department did not think he was strong enough for the promotion;
it did however make him a colonel in the Confederate Army. Finally it became evident that he could not again fight in Virginia,
and President Davis sent him abroad on a secret mission.

When Frank Robertson gave his friendship as he gave it to von
Borcke, he gave it without qualifications. He knew of course that
the big Prussian was not perfect, but he knew too that von Borcke
did not exaggerate his own bravery in the least, and he enjoyed his
companionship. As Stuart would tease the great Jackson, even so
could von Borcke make fun of Stuart, something no one else would
have dared to do. Captain Robertson (a photograph of him in
captain's uniform dated March 1865, is evidence that he was a captain before hostilities ceased) loved to tell how, after the Price diary with its effusions on the joys of student life in Germany and its
disagreeable remarks about the General had been published, Von
would love to roar, while getting ready for breakfast, "Oh, for Berlin!" Stuart did not think it was funny.[12]

Returning to Robertson's recollections of his adventures following von Borcke's wounding:

> The General made his headquarters in Paris that night [June
> 21]. Near midnight he and his staff rode out on the road to Upperville.
> We came to an infantry picket. The General asked if there was not a
> cavalry picket in their front. They said their orders were to fire upon
> anything approaching from that direction. The General seemed to
> think this strange and promptly sent me down the road to investi-
> gate. It was as dark as possible and after riding half a mile, I deemed
> it safer to dismount and scout along the adjacent field. I butted into
> a paling fence. I hitched my horse, climbed over and discovered a
> house in the yard. I cautiously poked around until I found the front
> porch. As I went up the steps my sabre clanged and I distinctly heard
> low voices in the road a few yards off. I knocked at the door very
> softly, and a woman came with a candle, which I told her to take
> away quickly and send her husband. He came promptly, and I told
> him (knowing all people in that county were Southern) I was a Con-
> federate sent to find out if we had a Confederate picket on the road.
> He hurriedly whispered,"Go, go, there are Yankee pickets in the road
> in front, some of these have just left the house."
>
> I went, and again heard the low talk in the road. I suppose they
> had seen the candle come and go. I crawled gently over the paling,
> and led my horse for some distance through the fields as I had done
> earlier. After I had taken the road back on my horse, I was startled

by the click of muskets. I called out, "Friend," and rode up and asked if they did not know a man had been sent down that road. They said they had just relieved the post, and that nothing had been said to them except to fire on anybody approaching. This was inexcusable certainly, and I barely missed being shot by them, a victim of simple ignorance and carelessness. I believe General Stuart was convinced we had a cavalry picket at the front as usual, as he was evidently puzzled by the report and orders of the first picket. Had I not dismounted and taken to the field, I would have ridden into a heavy Yankee picket on the road in front of the house, and then came near being shot by our own picket of some fifteen infantrymen when returning. These conditions caused me some resentment.

The General was asleep when I got back to headquarters and I never mentioned the subject to him afterwards. It would have caused an investigation, and our men and officers were tired and harassed by an all day fight.[13] Some cavalry officer was responsible for having no cavalry picket posted, while the picket officer would have got into trouble for not instructing the officer in charge of the relief picket.

The Yanks left early the next day [June 22], and our General and staff rode back over the ground fought over a few days before. Von Borcke with his bad wound in the neck we found near Upperville.

In the fighting of June 17, 19, and 21, Stuart lost 65 killed, 279 wounded, and 186 missing, a total of 510. The Federal losses were 82 killed, 336 wounded, and 465 missing for a total of 883; and not one Yank got through the Rebel screen.[14]

Once Pleasonton withdrew, Stuart turned his attention to the cavalry's role in the northern invasion. Considerable controversy exists as to Stuart's motivation for what became his third ride around a Federal army. With confusing orders from Lee and the urging of Longstreet not to give away the Confederate army's plans by following the rest of the army west of the mountains Stuart eventually decided to take the

General Robert E. Lee.

route in rear of the enemy.[15] Accordingly, the brigades of Wade Hampton, Fitz Lee, and Rooney Lee (the last named commanded still by Colonel Chambliss) assembled the evening of the 24th at Salem (now known as Marshall). Stuart left Grumble Jones, reputedly the best outpost officer in his command, Beverly Robertson, and two brigadiers who had been long on duty in the Valley, Albert G. Jenkins[16] and John Imboden,[17] with General Lee.

Robertson told of his part in his memoirs:

> The next thing I remember we were riding along the Upperville-Middleburg road with two or three brigades of cavalry [Hampton's, Fitz Lee's, and Rooney Lee's] following us. I think we camped one night before crossing the river.[18] We found a ford, bad and crooked, some eighteen miles above Washington; I don't remember the name of it. [It was Rowser's Ford.] We crossed at night. Artillery ammunition was distributed among the men to tote. Our light horse artillery and caissons nearly disappeared beneath the water.

All of the Army of Northern Virginia was across the river by this time, the morning of June 28,—all that is except for the brigades of Grumble Jones and Beverly Robertson. Jenkins and Imboden had accompanied General Lee with the main body of the Army. Ewell was nearing Harrisburg. Maj. Gen. Robert E. Rodes and Maj. Gen. Edward Johnson were at Carlisle, and Lt. Gen. Jubal A. Early had reached York. That day at Chambersburg Longstreet was to learn from his favorite spy that the Army of the Potomac had also crossed the river and was in the neighborhood of Frederick, Maryland and that Maj. Gen. Joseph "Fighting Joe" Hooker had been replaced by Maj. Gen. George G. Meade. This data he promptly turned over to General Lee in the same town. Robertson recorded:

> We reached the Maryland side about daylight and scattered in the fields. It was refreshing to watch the canal boats come gliding innocently and unexpectedly into these sleepy Rebs. I was lying only a few steps from the canal when one packet, well loaded with Yankee officers and many ladies, came trotting in. The astonishment, if nothing more, of the passengers when they saw hundreds of Rebs filling the landscape was intensely interesting. They stared blankly at us as they passed on to where we had a committee at work giving paroles and burning freight boats. We were in no shape to handle prisoners, so the passengers proceeded joyously to Washington, the gorgeously uniformed officers with paroles in their pockets. All the other boats, including one or two loaded with whiskey, were burned.
>
> After breakfast, so to speak, Boots and Saddles was sounded and we headed towards Washington. Our advance scouts soon re-

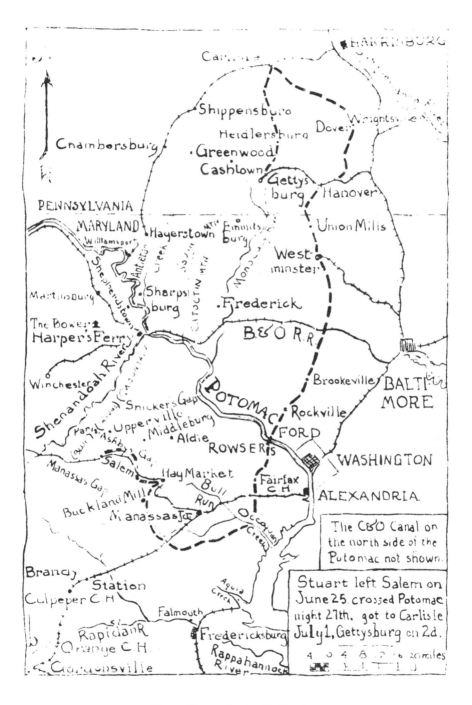

Stuart's route to Gettysburg.

ported a regiment of Federal cavalry coming our way on the same road. A very hilarious crowd they were for much boisterous noise did resound through the pine woods. Here came the innocent Yanks,—they were the "pack ups," gathered around Washington and being sent to the front. They were quite close but, from the nature of the road, not in sight when the General ordered the first squadron of the 4th Virginia, already waiting with drawn sabres, to charge. Then resounded the Rebel Yell. Not a shot was fired, but these happy, gallant eight hundred in blue did proceed with much celerity to seek the City of Washington, some twenty miles away. Except for a few sabre cuts, little damage was done. We took about a dozen prisoners.[19]

The column moved on leisurely for a space. Then, as we approached Rockville, learning that the Washington City Quartermaster Train was just beyond coming up from the Capital on its way to Frederick, a gallop was ordered for the advance squadron of the 2nd South Carolina Cavalry, Lieutenant Thomas Lee commanding. Down through the streets of Rockville we went with a rush, General Stuart and staff riding close to the rear of the advance. Ladies came to the doors and windows, and handkerchiefs of greeting and sympathy were waved on all sides.

Reaching the hill south of Rockville, we caught sight of the Washington City Train in retreat, 175 wagons with six matched mules to each. A circus was on that I have never seen paralleled. The race continued until within a few miles of Georgetown, and we gathered in 175 wagons and 1050 mules,—and this outfit with the exception of some overturned wagons, was safely delivered to General Lee's Army at Gettysburg. I firmly believe we could have captured Washington that day. But this was not on the programme, I suspect, and we returned to Rockville, where we loafed an hour or so.

Stuart's cavalry reached Rockville about noon on the 28th and spent the rest of the day paroling more than four hundred prisoners—a gesture which turned out to be a waste of time as the paroles were not honored. It was 5 o'clock the next afternoon when they got to Westminster, a distance of only about forty miles. Here Maj. Napoleon B. Knight with two companies of the 1st Delaware Cavalry disputed his passage with unquestionable valor. He lost 67 of 95 men. In capturing this important railhead, two of Stuart's lieutenants, Lt. St. Pierre Gibson of Co. D, and Lt. John William Murray of Co. E, both of the 4th Virginia Cavalry, were killed.[20] The men and horses were again well fed— the last time for many days—and the division moved out to spend the night at Union Mills.

From Rockville, we rode north towards York and through other towns not now remembered. We rode night and day, almost without rest, and I remember suffering much from want of sleep, food and water. We were much hampered by the long wagon train captured near Rockville, mules breaking down from fatigue, and acquiring Pennsylvania's big farm horses in place of them. We butt[ed] into Yankee cavalry at Hanover [on the 30th].

This was Kilpatrick's Division again, and the Federals threw the leading Confederate elements out of the town. With Fitz Lee on the flank and Wade Hampton behind many miles of wagon trains, Stuart could not get enough of his men together to defeat Kilpatrick. Without that wagon train, the Rebels would probably have passed Hanover, just fourteen miles due east of Gettysburg, before Kilpatrick arrived, and they might have established contact with Lee that day. The Southerners lingered just outside the town some hours, ready to burn the wagon train if need be, but Kilpatrick was satisfied merely to hold Hanover.[21] In the evening Stuart turned towards York. Learning that Early had already left there, he continued the march through the night, arriving in Dover the next morning, July 1. Thence he sent Major Reid Venable[22] and Captain Harry Lee[23] in search of Lee and Ewell. Stuart himself with the main body continued on to Carlisle. Robertson recalled the ride and the events at Carlisle that followed:

I was on Bostona instead of my favorite war horse Miranda. Bostona was about to collapse; so was The Garnett's horse, so we went horse-hunting in the woods. Finding a dozen or more hidden in the brush, we selected two, abandoned ours in place of them and rejoined the General. I rode my new mount for four days when she gave out and fell in the road at last. I managed to get into an advance guard skirmish and captured the worst-riding horse I ever was on. This U.S. branded horse could do naught but trot, and such a trot that I felt my brains would be addled.

It was a long and very trying trip as far north as Carlisle. Carlisle wasn't expecting us. We reached there about dark. General Stuart and staff rode halfway through the town before we were discovered to be the enemy. The streets were full of people; ladies, children and housemaids were much in evidence. Suddenly the presence of Rebels became known and then a stampede of course followed. Such a scurrying out of sight, and in a moment the street was bare.

Withdrawing a few hundred yards, General Stuart sent an officer and a bugler with a flag of truce demanding the surrender of the town. It was weird and peculiar to see this officer with a handkerchief tied to his sabre, followed by a bugler, go galloping into town, the latter blowing twice while the former brandished his handkerchief. The demand, as I remember, was to surrender or the town would be shelled. It seems that a full brigade of militia infantry was guarding the town, and a flat refusal came from the officer commanding. [Brigadier General William F. Smith, better known as "Baldy," replied, "Shell away."][24] We ran up a battery and shelled the town. After seeing all those ladies and children, I remember I somehow didn't like the crashing of shells among the houses. Suddenly a volley was fired upon us, a bullet striking a box tree by me.

I was very thirsty and went back a few blocks to a house with much shrubbery in front. I dismounted and knocked on the door of this handsome residence. No reply, so I walked in; nobody on the upper floor so I went down stairs. My knock was responded to by a very weak, "Come in." I walked into a big room and found fifteen or twenty people ranged around the wall, apparently awaiting death. I took off my hat and asked if I could have some water. I nearly emptied a bucketful while the panicked people looked on. Seeing that I was seemingly harmless, they asked if there was any danger from the cannonade then going on. I told them there was none: the guns were facing the other way, into the city.

Then we became quite sociable and I spent minutes talking to these people. They seemed surprised that I was a gentleman and meant them no harm. They became downright affectionate and presented me with a big plate of much needed food. Our parting was truly kindly and a handshake was given all around. I wish I could go back to that house and meet those people again.

After leaving my friends of the water bucket I went forward to the Horse Artillery Brigade, still firing on the city. There sat General Stuart. He immediately sent me to tell Colonel [Williams C.] Wickham of the 4th Virginia to burn the U. S. Barracks. Well, he pointed,— that was all he ever said. Following his point, I rode through sundry dark streets and byways, expecting every minute to have my head blown off from a window or door, and found Colonel Wickham and gave him his orders. In a few moments I saw the grand cavalry barracks begin to glow from many points and then, with a great burst of flame, light up the scenery for miles around. I was too sleepy and exhausted even to know how I got back to General Stuart.[25]

The officers who had been sent to Lee and Ewell got back to Stuart about nine that evening, July 1. They told him that the first day's fighting at Gettysburg was favorable to the Southern cause, but General Lee wanted him to come at once.

Our troopers were soon on the move again, though reeling in their saddles from exhaustion. I only remember when we reached Gettysburg the next morning I could hear cannonading south of us. I was nearly dead with fatigue and loss of sleep. I was riding my third horse since crossing the Potomac, my own Bostona, one I borrowed from a farm and lastly one captured in a picket scrimmage, and he was the meanest cuss I ever rode.

General Stuart with Fitz Lee and Chambliss arrived in Gettysburg the afternoon of the 2nd, but General Hampton was held up at Hunterstown to fight Kilpatrick again. "For eight days and nights," as McClellan wrote, "the troops had been marching incessantly. On the ninth night they rested within the shelter of the army, with a grateful sense of relief words cannot express."[26]

The next morning, July 3, "pursuant to instructions from the commanding general," said General Stuart in his official report, "I moved forward to a position on the left of General Ewell's left, and in advance of it, where a commanding ridge [Cress Ridge] completely controlled a wide plain of cultivated fields stretching towards Hanover, on the left, and reaching to the base of the mountain spurs, among which the enemy held positions. My command was increased by the addition of Jenkin's Brigade.... I moved this command and W. H. F. Lee's [under Colonel Chambliss] through the woods to a position, and hoped to effect a surprise upon the enemy's rear, but Hampton's and Fitz Lee's brigades, which had been ordered to follow me, unfortunately debouched into the open ground, disclosing the movement, and causing a corresponding movement of a large force of the enemy's cavalry. Having been informed that Generals Hampton and Lee were up, I sent for them to come forward, so that I could show them the situation at a glance from the elevated ground I held and arrange for further operations."[27]

On the afternoon of the third day of the Battle of Gettysburg, [Maj. Gen. George E.] Pickett was to lead his division up the west slope of Cemetery Ridge to immortal glory. Stuart was beyond the left flank of Ewell's Corps, which had constituted the left flank of the Confederate army up to that time. He was thus in a position to protect this flank if need arose. Stuart commented in his report that, "Had the enemy's main body been dislodged, as was confidently hoped and expected, I was in precisely the right position to discover it and improve the opportunity. I watched keenly and anxiously the indications in his rear for that purpose, while in the attack which I intended (which was forestalled by our troops being exposed to view), his cavalry would have been separated from the main body, and gave promise of solid results and advantages."[28]

About noon that day, between Stuart and Cemetery Ridge some three miles west, a stand of timber concealed parts of General David Gregg and General Judson Kilpatrick and their divisions. One of Kilpatrick's brigadiers was General George A. Custer, he of the long yellow curls and the beautiful velvet uniform. Custer had been about to take his four Michigan regiments to Meade's left, where trouble was expected, when they received word that a large body of Rebel cavalry was on the York turnpike headed east. Custer asked permission to stay put, and it was granted. The Confederates had no idea that two divisions of Federal cavalry, mounted on well-fed horses, were between them and the rear of Meade's line.

"In the afternoon (about 4:30 o'clock, I should think)," wrote General Hampton, "an order came from General Stuart for General Fitz Lee and myself to report to him, leaving our brigades where they were. Thinking that it would not be proper for both of us to leave the ground at the same time, I told General Lee that I would go to see General Stuart first, and on my return he could go. Leaving General Lee, I rode off to see General Stuart, but could not find him."[29] Robertson recalled the events leading up to the battle:

> I recall our cavalry was massed in woods [about three miles] east of Gettysburg, a very big field in front of us. The General and staff rode out of the woods to a cleared hill. A Yankee battery at the far end of the big clearing opened on us, and we rode back again. The General disappeared and the staff seemed scattered.
>
> A little later General Hampton asked me where General Stuart was. He said he had been trying in vain to find him. I also had been looking for him for some time, as were several members of his staff. General Hampton and his officers seemed excited. He told me, "You must find him and tell him that we have just captured a man belonging to the Sixth Army Corps, who stated that his corps had just arrived and gone into the Gettysburg breastworks. It is most important that General Stuart know this."
>
> This was a startling and unexpected reinforcement to Meade's army, already greatly outnumbering Lee's.[30] I followed a lane near which I had seen General Stuart an hour earlier; I passed entirely out of sight of our men and headed straight for the enemy, riding very cautiously and expecting every moment to strike a Yankee picket. After about a mile on this road parallel to the big field, I saw a man on a knoll behind a tree, his back to me, looking intently at something beyond. I recognized the General. I went up on the knoll to him and saw in the plain below what looked like 20,000 cavalry,—the whole country was black with them. The General seemed worried by

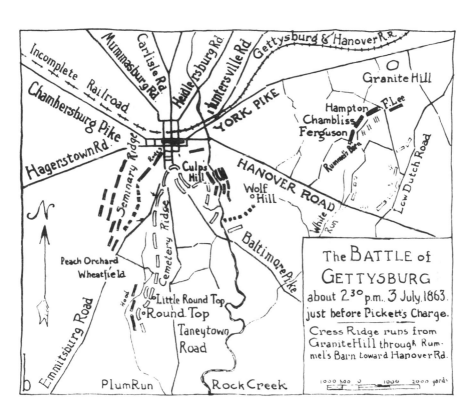

The Battle of Gettysburg · July 3, 1863.

my message and he ordered me to ride back as quickly as possible and tell General Hampton to keep his cavalry out of sight in the woods, and avoid an engagement.

Riding full speed I was yet too late: ere I reached the place I had left General Hampton, I saw him on a full charge across the field with three brigades of cavalry, meeting a charge of Yankee cavalry. The great field was covered with galloping horses, shouting men.

Continued General Hampton in his official report,

On my return to the field, I saw my brigade in motion, having been ordered to charge by General [Fitzhugh] Lee. This order I countermanded, as I did not think it a judicious one, and the brigade resumed its former position, not, however, without loss, as the movement had disclosed its position to the enemy. A short time after this, an officer from Colonel Chambliss reported to me that he had been sent to ask support from General Lee, but that he had replied that my brigade was nearest and should support Chambliss' brigade. Seeing that support was essential, I sent Colonel

[Laurence S.] Baker[31] [1st North Carolina Cavalry], ordering him to send two regiments to protect Chambliss, who had made a charge (I know not by whose orders), and who was falling back before a large force of the enemy. The First North Carolina and the Jeff Davis Legion were sent Colonel Baker, and these regiments drove back the enemy; but in their eagerness they followed him too far, and encountered his reserve in heavy force. Seeing the state of affairs at this juncture, I rode rapidly to the front, to take charge of these two regiments, and, while doing this, to my surprise I saw the rest of my brigade (except the Cobb Legion) and Fitz Lee's brigade charging. In the hand-to-hand fighting which ensued, as I was endeavoring to extricate the First North Carolina and the Jeff Davis Legion, I was wounded and had to leave the field, after turning over the command to Colonel Baker.[32]

Earlier Robertson had attached himself to Lieutenant Colonel Vincent Witcher's battalion [34th Virginia Cavalry] of Jenkins' Brigade.[33] They held the Rummel Barn and the stone fence which extended from it to the right.

Jenkins' cavalry was dismounted and lining a stone fence running parallel with the charging masses and were busily engaged in emptying saddles as the Yanks passed by a hundred yards off. My order being quashed, I sat behind Jenkins' line and viewed the combat, the only one I ever truly enjoyed.

Our three brigades charged in echelon, encountering great masses of Federal cavalry, and a grand melee followed. All was chaos in a few minutes: looked like two huge clouds, Gray and Blue, chasing each other to and fro across the big field. Jenkins' men had nothing to do but blaze away as the Blue Cloud passed by them, being protected by the stone fence or wall, and they did great execution; the Yankees seemed too much occupied with their front to care about their flank. Though hundreds passed us, and but a few yards off at times, I did not see a man fire at us or even look our way.

At one time the 1st Virginia Cavalry (of Fitz Lee's Brigade) captured one of the enemy's batteries, but could not hold it. Our men were greatly outnumbered and were sadly handicapped by exhausted horses, not to mention their own worn-out condition. I distinctly saw General Hampton on his grand sorrel in the midst of the fray where he was both shot and sabred. Though the sabre slash fractured his skull, General Hampton survived this battle and was able to returned to full military duty; he survived the War a number of years.

This cavalry fight occurred on the extreme left of our lines. Neither side seemed to gain any permanent advantage, but followed each other back and forth in general disorder. These charges and counter-charges lasted perhaps an hour. I watched for the General, who I suspected would follow my course, but I did not see him again until after the fighting was over; this was apparently by mutual consent.

H. B. McClellan's account of this action, while going into greater detail, is in agreement with Robertson's. He concluded his description with this sentence: "Stuart had no fresh troops with which to renew the fight; he herefore maintained his position until night, when he withdrew to the York turnpike, leaving the 1st Virginia on picket on the field."[34] Admittedly, in the context of the entire battle, this was not a very important affair, and contrary to the opinion of some, it resulted in a draw.

The real reason that the cavalry fight on the extreme left of Lee's front appears unimportant is that it was so completely overshadowed by Pickett's charge that same afternoon. Robertson wrote:

We could not see the great infantry fight going on, on our right but I remember the very leaves on the trees seemed to tremble and vibrate from the tremendous thunder of three hundred guns. They say the rumpus was heard in Washington and Baltimore. As all now know, our assaults were repulsed. We undertook the impossible. I saw the task given Pickett's Division and even wondered as a boy, and still do as a man, how any human being could have been expected to take that Gettysburg hill, lined with stone fences and breastworks, and every inch covered with men and guns. There was something about that charge of the Virginians that is a mystery, that all explanations have failed in my mind to explain. Someone was at fault, but I don't believe it was General Lee. The confidence of the Confederate army in him was infinite. What he said was law and right, from officers to the most homesick conscripts. But it is today a mystery and a problem with the same devoted troops of General Lee as to why he expected and demanded the impossible. It really looked as if our grand old chief had suddenly become demented, and his best friends and these same devoted troops will ever wonder and wonder—but never, never doubt or lose faith in Uncle Robert. That the Confederate Army at Gettysburg collided with the impossible, no soldier doubts today,— and then and there their cause was irreparably lost.

While, of course, we failed in defeating the Federals, it is an acknowledged fact that we quietly marched back to Virginia almost undisturbed and at our leisure. There was nothing of the rout that follows defeat, and the pursuit of "the victorious army of Meade" was scarcely noticeable.[35]

On July 4, the recalcitrant Confederate Army waited west of Seminary Ridge. Meade held his army in place on the eminence where their losses had been almost as great as those of the attacking Southerners. It began to rain. Lack of ammunition, lack of food, lack of everything necessary to an army except valor, made it necessary for Lee to retreat. That afternoon Meade sent Buford and Kilpatrick south to wreck Lee's wagon trains that would have to come down the Cumberland Valley ahead of his army. The brigades of Jones and Robertson left in Virginia had been ordered north on June 30; they had covered the hundred and fifty miles in three days and were with the main army again. That night Lee began his retreat to Virginia. When he reached the Potomac River crossings at Williamsport, he found the incessant rains that had already slowed his progress made it impossible for him to cross.

There were many minor cavalry brushes, but Frank Robertson wrote not a word about them. He was probably too dog-tired, too wolf-hungry to remember anything about them. Scanty rations were issued to the men, but nothing at all in the line of food was provided for the Confederate officers. "For four or five days in succession," remembered Major McClellan, "we received our only food after nightfall at the hands of a young lady in Hagerstown, whose father, a Southerner, sympathized with the Confederacy."[36]

Robertson's memoir recounted his experiences on the retreat:

> We reached Hagerstown O. K., our cavalry following and protecting the rear of our retreating army. Breastworks were thrown up around the town, and we awaited an attack. I was sent by General Stuart with a message to General Lee. I wrote it in my pocketbook and also in my memory. It was to tell him that picket lines were established and that the cavalry—men and horses—were exhausted, and that the latter needed rest and shoeing.
>
> I found General Lee sitting alone in a piece of woods. There was not a staff officer nor anybody around except a lone courier, who held my horse during the interview. Marse Robert greeted me in a kindly, almost fatherly way, and said, "Come, boy, what news of the cavalry?"
>
> He made me sit down on a camp stool, and sitting down himself after I had delivered my message, he proceeded to ask me all about cavalry matters generally. I posted him as well as I could and with a large amount of embarrassment, but no father ever talked more gently or sweetly to his son than Uncle Robert did to me. I was ragged and haggard no doubt, and he seemed to appreciate it and to feel for me as an exponent of his many thousand played-out soldiers. He looked worn and tired, but his eyes blazed with energy and he seemed to me as nobly and as splendidly defiant and confident as ever,—I

had seen him many times before, in and out of battle. The conference lasted about twenty minutes. I remember especially his last remark, "There will be no rest for man or beast until we whip these people!"

This saying I repeated at General Stuart's headquarters that evening, and we thought then that there would be a big fight the next day. But I had not been back at headquarters in half an hour before General Stuart told me to go to Colonel [Milton J.] Ferguson, commanding Jenkins' brigade, "Tell him to move his men into the breastworks as soon as the infantry move out." I knew this meant a retreat. When I reached Jenkins' brigade, the infantry were slipping back in squads from the line, and Ferguson at once deployed his men and scattered them among the deserted works.

That night [July 13], General Stuart and staff rode along this cavalry line substitute and his couriers sang songs with sham confidence to let the unsuspecting enemy believe our lines were full and longing for attack. It was raining and very dark. The river was very high.

We had barely reached the suburbs of Williamsport about 9 PM when the General ordered me to go to the lower ford with some message to our headquarters ambulance. It was important, but to this day I have never been able to remember what it was. I had never been to Williamsport, nor had I any idea where the lower ford was, but I rode down the black street at a fast gallop. I saw a big fire ahead that flashed upon the river; it blinded both Miranda and me, so without pause we went over the abutment of a bridge across the canal. We plunged into space. I fell a mile it seemed, and I thought thoughts galore. The next thing I remember I was lying on my back pulling mud out of my mouth, and Miranda was standing beside me. We had fallen about thirty feet. I remained there I suppose for an hour as everything seemed whirling around. I wasn't sure I was alive. I must have been unconscious for some time as I have no recollection of hitting bottom or getting to the opposite bank. My right shoulder was badly damaged.

I went to the ford, found the ambulance, bore patiently the jeers and laughter of a lot of soldiers around the fire, "Where the hell did you come from?" etc. I was a mess of mud, Miranda ditto. I led her out into the river and washed the mud off her and soaked it off me. I lost nothing in the accident but my hat.

After my bath I rode back another way home. I saw some cavalry in a furniture shop, and they allowed me to make one more. I pulled out the lower drawer of a bureau and went to sleep in it. The next morning I called for help to get out of it,—there was an inch of muddy water left in it. I also had to be lifted on to Miranda,—very stiff and right shoulder hurting.

I reported to General Stuart whom I found just starting to cross at the upper ford. I was sent back immediately to call in the rear guard. I didn't tell the General how used up I was, so I went back and met the rear guard on the hill above the town. They didn't need any orders,—they were coming full tilt with lots of Yankees following.

The mud was deep at the upper ford so I was afraid my used-up steed would stick in it as twenty or more horses had done, so I went to the lower ford alone. Not a soul in sight, but I saw some wagons in the middle of the river. I supposed they were on the ford and headed for them. Miranda plunged head under and commenced swimming, lifted again on a ledge, then another plunge. I unhooked my sabre and dropped it in the river, expecting I might have to swim myself. I found the wagons half-submerged, mules hanging dead in their harness. They must have been far below the ford, and were probably still being carried downstream.

Just then Mr. Yank began firing at me, and I wasn't happy. Balls splashing all around. After sundry deep plunges we reached the Virginia shore, only to find a line of rocks some two or three feet about the water, making it impossible for Miranda to get out. I got off and led her down the river perhaps fifty yards, bullets getting livelier and closer, when I found a place where the little mare could scuffle out.

I managed to mount again and then I joined General Stuart and staff on top of a hill watching the Yanks beyond Williamsport. A battery opened and killed several men in a cavalry regiment near us. It seemed hard indeed to be thus laid low just as we felt we had got home again.

An ambulance appeared, full of ladies; they had just crossed and they were scared. The General sent me to ask if they had passports. They hadn't, of course. I never reported, and on they went.

I was so stiff and miserable that I didn't know much of anything until we were on a hill opposite a great clearing on the north side of the river. Six or more guns were bush-covered and trained on this open field, men lying under their guns. We could hear musketry on the opposite side and soon a brigade of infantry appeared, moving in line at the double quick, followed by a heavy skirmish line firing as they came. Then an interval of a hundred or so yards; then a dense mass of Yanks appeared in pursuit, much cheering and some shouting. Our men had disappeared and were crossing the river on pontoons. I suppose 1800 Yanks were half way down the hill when our artillerymen jumped up and opened fire. I never enjoyed any sight more than the hasty retreat of those 1800 Yanks. I don't know about the execution, but I saw several men fly up the dust of exploding shells striking among them.

The next thing I remember we confronted a Yankee force at Shepherdstown. Things were quiet and General Stuart remarked, "I believe those Yanks have gone," and immediately galloped towards a stone fence. I followed, and perhaps some others. When we were about a hundred yards away, a skirmish line fired from the fence. The General wheeled his horse and returned to the point we had started from. A bullet cut his oilcloth, but I thought his escape wonderful as perhaps twenty men fired at him and he was some distance in front of his escort. I happened, which was rare, to be riding by him on our return to camp, and I remarked upon his narrow escape. He replied, and I was struck with the unusual sadness of his voice, "Well, I expect to be killed ere this war ends."

We camped that night, the 15th, at the Bower, the home of the Dandridges, a beautiful place with many fine oak trees in front of the dwelling.[37] I was lying under them, rain pouring. The General came along, stopped and said, "Poor little fellow, I will send you to the house." Two couriers appeared and escorted me there where I was put to bed and, my, how good that bed did feel,—I hadn't been in one for many weeks. I couldn't move for two days. Dr. Eliason looked me over, didn't examine that shoulder, and sent me home on a two-month furlough. Two days later a government ambulance came for me and took me to Salem on the Virginia and Tennessee railroad, two hundred and ten miles up the Valley of Virginia. Major Bell [Dabney Ball],[38] a fighting preacher of our cavalry, rode with me, while Sam followed with my horses Miranda and Yank. I traveled this entire distance in a big hair-covered rocking chair Major Bell [Ball] was taking to his wife in Salem. We lived high on partridges which I killed from the ambulance with my cavalry pistol as they sat on the stone fences lining the road.

I left Miranda with Judge Brockenbrough[39] in Lexington, while Sam rode my Yankee steed on to Abingdon. He was a tough old brute and kicked viciously at anyone attempting to mount him on his right side. I gave him afterwards to Lieutenant Taylor of Kentucky, whose horse was stolen from the Meadows stable one night while he was my guest. He rode him to the trans-Mississippi department.

Stuart's cavalry still had plenty of fight left in the fall of 1863, and Frank Robertson must have regretted missing the "Buckland Races" of October 19. Stuart lured the enemy cavalry, led by Custer, Kilpatrick, and Davies, after him until Fitz Lee was in a position to fall upon their flank. Stuart then turned and joined in pursuing the Yanks some five miles. It was the last time they were able to enjoy their pristine sport of making the Yankees skedaddle.[40]

7

The Shattering

The right wing of the Army of the Potomac crossed the Rapidan at Germanna Ford again on May 4, 1864. The army corps of Maj. Gen. John Sedgwick and Maj. Gen. Gouverneur K. Warren, accompanied by their long wagon trains under snow-white covers, marched over on good pontoon bridges.[1] A little further to the east at Ely's Ford, Maj. Gen. Winfield S. Hancock and Maj. Gen. Ambrose E. Burnside with the rest of 118,000 men were also crossing.[2] In immediate command of this sixth "On to Richmond" campaign was General George G. Meade, hero of Gettysburg, but he was under the newly appointed general-in-chief of all the Federal armies, General Ulysses S. Grant, hero of the West, who was with the Army of the Potomac for the first time.

To their surprise, Lee had allowed the invading army to cross the river unhindered; he allowed them to get well into the Wilderness of Spotsylvania before he attacked them on the 5th with Ewell and Hill. The next morning Longstreet with his veteran First Corps arrived, and they were promptly thrown in. A little later, just when it seemed that the Rebels were about to roll up the flank of the Yankee army in as great a disaster as they had inflicted some three miles north of that spot a year earlier, Longstreet was wounded. Like Jackson, he was shot by his own men while making a personal reconnaissance in front of the Confederate line.

The Wilderness was well named. Trees stunted from overcrowding and dense undergrowth, all matted together with wild vines, made it hard to see fifteen yards in any direction, and even harder for man or horse to get through the brush. This year, unlike the spring of 1863, there had been little rain, and everything was tinder dry. More than two thousand Northerners were killed in the first two days, and more than five times that many wounded. The dead leaves and undergrowth caught fire and again, for the wounded unable to walk, it was a question of whether the stretcher-bearers would reach them before the flames did; the fires were much worse than the year before.

The Army of Northern Virginia was hungry and barefoot, but it had a tradition to maintain. These men had routed McDowell that day in July 1861, when they, not the Federals, had called themselves the Army of the Potomac; they had whipped McClellan at the gates of Richmond, and had trounced the vainglorious Pope; they had stopped Burnside in a bloody repulse at Fredericksburg, and had beaten Hooker ingloriously. These commanders had all retreated promptly after their big battle, and the Rebels believed they could whip the best the North could send against them. But the new general did not play that way. Grant just moved by the left flank to a new position.

It is not planned here to follow Grant through Spotsylvania Court House and the Bloody Angle to Second Cold Harbor where he lost so many thousand men the morning of June 3, nor to tell again the story of his constant shifting to the left, nor of his incessant hammering at the Rebel army. Soon Grant had lost more men than Lee had in all at the beginning of the campaign, but Grant's men and supplies were inexhaustible. Lee's were not.

For some months after Frank Robertson got home to the Meadows, in August 1863, the records are scant. Being with the family he had no reason to write to them, and life was too dull for his later memoirs. One does find that on August 29, "Dr. Jno. G. Pride, Surgeon C. S." certified that he had carefully examined "F. S. Robertson, Lt. Engineer Corps, Genl. Stuart's command," and had found him "unable to perform the duties of a soldier because of Endocarditis." General Stuart himself on September 21 addressed him as "Lieutenant," corroborating that he had been again commissioned after Gettysburg.

A second-hand account of life at the Meadows that fall is given in a letter from Bessie Nicholas:[3]

> Great Grandma Charlotte had 4 sons and 2 daughters, Jane my grandma, and aunt Clara. One of Great Grandma's sons was the butler at The Meadows, either Steve or Alec, and he saved The Mead-

ows silver. When they knew the Yankees were coming, he buried it in the branch to keep them from taking it.

What pa loved to tell us most was when the Yankees were coming. His mistress had him watch for them. They asked him where his master was. He said in Richmond. They told him to say that. Mrs. Robertson stayed in the house. Where was the horses and Mrs. R. said, Frank show the men where the horses are. They were in the meadow, and the men caught the best horses and rode off on them." No wonder Frank Nicholas (who was always proud of having been named for Frank Robertson) loved to recall his importance when he, an eight-year-old slave-boy, acted as intermediary between his mistress and the invaders!

The Yankees told the slaves to come and get what they wanted, because they were burning the depot the next day. Some were afraid to go. But grandfather and Uncle Ben Evin hauled all night. They got Flour, Sugar, Coffee and many other things. The last load they had so much the tongue broke before they got home. They sold their master most of the things, but they kept some. The next day pa said They watched the Court House and the depot burn from the porch on top of the house at the Meadows.

The winter of 1863-1864 saw extensive reorganization in the Army of Northern Virginia. Stuart's cavalry was converted into a corps, though its first commander was not promoted. Wade Hampton and Fitz Lee became major generals, in August, and when Rooney Lee was finally exchanged[4] in March 1864, he too was promoted to major general (Col. Chambliss, who had handled his brigade so well from the time Lee was wounded at Brandy Station, had long been made a brigadier). It is true that the new divisions had usually only two brigades, and these brigades were rarely as big as a regiment had been two years earlier. The war had been taking a heavy toll, and General Stuart must have been getting lonesome. When Captain Blackford was transferred to a newly organized regiment of engineers in February 1864, with the rank of major (the tables of organization did not permit the cavalry corps to have an engineer officer with a rank higher than captain), John Esten Cooke[5] was the only officer left of those who had constituted Stuart's official family when Blackford first joined it.[6]

Lieutenant Robertson probably reported to General Stuart in his camp near Culpeper in March, judging from a letter he wrote his father from Richmond April 5, 1864:

> I have allowed more time to elapse than intended without writing you, but have really been very busily engaged in making several maps of the country along the Rapidan, for General Stuart and [Brig.

Gen. James B.] Gordon ever since my return.[7] I finished them yesterday and will forward them at once, as they are very much needed at present....

General Stuart seemed very glad to see me and of his own accord promised to write immediately to Col. [Alfred L.] Rives and have me promoted, if possible.[8] I am glad to hear so little damage to the place has resulted from Longstreet's proximity. It is generally reported and believed here he will shortly rejoin Lee with the greater part of his command, leaving Buckner and Morgan in charge of the remainder.

How are my horses looking?—is either fit for service? If Miranda's leg will admit of it, I would rather have her than any other.... As all Corps Staff will be allowed the usual number, I will still have two. If you can manage to send my banjo, I would love to have it.

That April Robertson may have been the only engineer on Stuart's staff.

> Hd Qrs Cav Corps A. N. Va.
> April 19th, 1864.

Dear Frank:

I send you a map, of the battle of Chancellorsville which I wish you to reduce to letter size, two copies. I am anxious to have it as soon as possible. Preserve the map as it is particularly valuable. Please give my sincere regards to your Father's family, and my condolences to Blackford[9] for the bereavement he has suffered.

> Very truly yours,
> J. E. B. Stuart

In after years his second commission as lieutenant did not seem very important to Robertson for he did not mention it in either version of his memoirs, but in 1864 rank was terribly important to him. He felt with justification that he deserved promotion at least to first lieutenant. In Richmond he soon received another letter, dated April 30, from the Headquarters of the Cavalry Corps; this one was from his old tentmate, "The" Garnett.

Dear Frank,

Genl. Stuart has just now requested me to inform you that he has received a communication from Col. Rives stating that your application will be presented to Genl. [Maj. Gen. Jeremy F.] Gilmer as soon as possible for his favorable consideration.

I received your note sent by Woodbridge, and have sent one of those maps to Genl. Gordon. You must excuse me for not informing you of this before. I trust that you[r] promotion may be soon made now, and that you will be able to join us in the coming campaign.

There is no news of any kind up here;—we are all even more quiet than we were two weeks ago.

Remember me kindly to your family and believe me,

Your sincere friend
Theodore S. Garnett, Jr.

Little did Theodore Garnett think that the ball would begin in another four days! For Robertson, still at Richmond, where he had been sent by Stuart to work at the Engineer Bureau on maps of the Battle of Chancellorsville, the news of his promotion was too good to contain and on May 5 he wrote to his father about it and his horses which needed to be sent so he could join General Stuart in the field.

Dear Pa,

I am as well as I probably will be, & am anxious to return as soon as possible. If transportation by R.R. can be had, I would like my horses sent down at once—if it cannot be obtained, you may possibly find some soldier coming down to join the County Company, whence Sam could accompany. I do not think it safe to trust his coming alone & rather than run the risk, had best start from home myself. If they can be sent to Richmond by R.R., a bag or two of corn (if it be had), I should like sent to sustain them a few days while getting over the stiffness incidental to transportation by R.R. My sabre & gum coat are the only articles I shall require from home—the latter is in my chest in the office—there is also an old pair of cavalry boots in it, which you can give to the boy who brings the horses.

Tell Sam to see that my bridle, saddle & halter are in good order before starting. I am afraid to trust to Miranda's leg—Minna [?] will suit as well I think, unless you have some special use for her—also one of the small bay work horses.

Many rumors are afoot about the movements of Lee & Grant & it is generally believed heavy fighting is going on today. I saw Mr. Carter Lee just now on the street.[10] He says he has heard nothing authentic from the army today. He told me it was reported & believed that Newbern [New Berne] N.C. had been evacuated & our troops in possession.[11] A brigade of Tennessee troops from about _____ [word illegible] are passing thro' town this morning. All the troops about Richmond I hear have been ordered to Lee.

Your letter to Kate has just arrived & tho' she regrets the loss of the turkey, is overjoyed to hear you will soon join us. I hope this letter will reach you in time to attend to my matters before starting. Gen. Stuart sent me word, his application for my promotion had been approved by Col. Rives & forwarded to Col. [Maj. Gen.] Gilmer.

> In haste, your affec son
> Frank

All send their love—Kate says she will answer your letter very soon. Please let me know at once what arrangements can be made about my horses. Enclosed you will find the key of my chest.

Robertson's horses would not arrive in time, and he never rode with Stuart again. Events were moving toward a fateful encounter about six miles northeast of Richmond near a small crossroads named Yellow Tavern.

Stuart and his cavalry were engaged with the Yankees in the Wilderness on May 5, for the most part fighting on foot with the Rebel infantry. On the 6th, Meade, not appreciating the power of cavalry used en masse as cavalry, was overruled by Grant who gave Phil Sheridan his head. Sheridan then assembled behind the front, in the vicinity of Fredericksburg, all his troopers (more than twelve thousand men, armed with the new repeating carbine, and their horses in excellent condition) and thirty-two pieces of artillery, for another raid on Richmond. This was by far the biggest force ever sent by the North on such a mission. In later years Robertson recalled Sheridan's threat to Richmond:

> I was working on the Chancellorsville maps one day, May 10, when the alarm bell sounded. All furloughed or other soldiers in Richmond were ordered to Capitol Square and formed into companies for the breastworks as the Yanks were coming. I joined an Artillery company. We marched to South Richmond and manned a battery of stationary guns [for Maj. Gen. Benjamin Butler still had a sizeable army down the James]. The next day we heard heavy firing on the north side of Richmond. Willie Worthington's mother sent a boy on a horse with a basket of provisions for him. We asked the old general commanding to allow us to take it to a shady clump of bushes. After consuming the good food, we both mounted the horse and deserted for Richmond. The boy was left to follow with the basket. We ran the bridge picket of old citizens.
>
> We went to the Arsenal on Seventh Street and procured muskets and cartridges and went out to our front lines, sort of foot loose and under our own command. We ran into another fellow pretty much similarly situated. We three started out for the skirmish line outside the breastworks, when a bullet struck a gatepost we were standing by, and the three guardsmen thought they had no business beyond the breastworks, and, things quieting down, they bravely marched back to town.

Getting home the evening of May 12, I heard that Stuart had been badly wounded the evening before at Yellow Tavern, and had been taken to the home of his brother-in-law, Dr. Charles Brewer, in Richmond. I went there at once to find my dear General dying from a carbine ball through his body.[12] Dr. John B. Fontaine,[13] his staff surgeon, who was also to be killed a few months later, was the only other member of his staff I remember seeing in the room. I thought General Stuart recognized me when I went to the bedside. Half an hour later he drew up his leg, saying, "Oh, me," and quickly died.[14] His wife did not arrive from the country till too late to see him alive.

Thus passed beyond question the greatest cavalry leader of that war, perhaps of modern times. He was singularly alert, night and day, and his dash and high courage were an inspiration and encouragement to his devoted troopers, than whom no finer body of horse ever existed, I believe.

J. E. B. Stuart had been thirty-one hardly three months when, after two days of facing fearful odds, he received his death wound. But he had saved Richmond from falling into Sheridan's hands. With a force not a third as large, he had harassed the powerful Federal column of superbly equipped, superbly mounted men to such an extent "that they gave up the game without ever reaching the fortifications of the city."[15]

Of all the tributes that poured forth none was more sincere than that from his old enemy, Brigadier General William E. Jones, soon himself to fall on the field of battle beyond the Blue Ridge, "By God, Martin![16] You know I had little love for Stuart, and he had just as little for me; but that is the greatest loss that army has ever sustained except the death of Jackson!"[17] Following Stuart's death Robertson found himself reassigned.

Three of his staff, Major [Andrew] Reid Venable, The' Garnett and I were ordered to report to General Rooney Lee, middle son of Marse Robert and commander of a division of cavalry, two brigades of Virginians and one of North Carolinians. Garnett became Provost-Marshal and I served as Engineer Officer to this division until the surrender at Appomattox.

Our division vibrated between the right and left of Lee's army, extending behind the breastworks from some miles south of Petersburg on across the James to the defenses of Richmond. There were many heavy skirmishes in which our division fought, generally dismounted. In one of these Bob Turner[18] and Bob Lee[19] were both wounded, the former so badly he never returned to us. Both belonged to our Boy's Mess. Turner and myself were sitting side by side on our horses when he was struck by a shell, and half his back raked off it seemed. I caught him and called to General Lee (W.H.F.) that Bob (Turner) was wounded. He replied, "Take him to the rear" which I did, holding him with difficulty in the saddle until an ambulance was found. I never saw him afterwards. He was a splendid soldier, and we greatly missed him. Bob Lee, with his slightly wounded arm, was soon back in camp again.

I may mention that while riding the road to Petersburg July 30, 1864, I witnessed the immense explosion on the Crater, perhaps a mile off. The column of smoke and dust rose to a great height and with it some two hundred men and a battery of artillery.

Now that Robertson was actively on campaign again his letters to his family resumed. They provide more detail than his reminiscences concerning his activities at this time. He wrote to his father on August 5, 1864:

Here we are again in the vicinity of Petersburg and not more than a mile from our old camp. On crossing the James [River] last Sunday night the division was ordered to return to their old position, but was afterwards halted several miles north of Petersburg to await further orders. There we remained until yesterday anxiously expecting to be ordered to the Valley to reinforce [Lt. Gen. Jubal A.] Early[20] as it was generally reported that some of the cavalry were to be ordered there. We were doomed to disappointment however and yesterday evening were marched back to picket our old line of 4 or 5 miles extending from the infantry lines to Gen. Fitz Lee's Division. He in turn connects with Hampton who occupies the extreme right of our lines.

Everything is perfectly quiet along the lines, and I think it probable we may remain here for some time. We have been very busy all morning in fixing up our new camp. It is better located than any we have had, but the weather is so intensely warm, the water so indifferent and the flies so troublesome, that one finds it difficult to enjoy life under any circumstances. Lizards and snakes abound to an alarming extent—only yesterday I found an immense scorpion in quiet possession of my blanket. I have no doubt he had been my bedfellow all night.

Maj. Venable has just come in from Petersburg and states that it was reported that large bodies of troops Cavalry and Artillery were moving all last night towards our extreme right. I presume we'll make but short stay at our newly rigged HdQrs.

My horses have both fallen off considerably. The immense distance now necessary to haul forage prevents its regular issue and there being no grass in this county and the corn ration light, they are obliged to suffer. My health has been first rate until the past few days. I have felt a few sharp pains in one of my arms, and considerable uneasiness about my head. I feel no apprehensions however of any serious attack. I have written mostly to let you all hear from me and am sorry I can give you no news. My love to all. Ma's letter reached me yesterday.

Robertson was correct in that he was not to remain long in his "newly rigged camp." By August 18, when he wrote his sister, he was camped near White Tavern six miles east of Richmond.

I have had no chance to drop you a few lines since we left Petersburg and now I have with difficulty borrowed a candle to write by, fearing I may have no other opportunity shortly.

We crossed to the north side of the James last Sunday (14th) and have been busy fighting and marching ever since. Monday we drove the enemy several miles when they rallied and drove us back about a mile. During the fight Bob Lee was wounded in the arm. Tuesday the enemy attacked in force and after sharp fighting our line broke and in attempting to rally it, Gen. Chambliss was killed and left in the hands of the enemy. We continued to retire before greatly superior numbers until [Brig. Gen. Rufus] Barringer's[21] brigade came up when a stand was successfully made and there we remained until Brig. Gen. [Martin] Gary[22] connected with our right. A charge was then ordered and the cav. dismounted and in line of battle as Infantry rushed into the woods with a yell, which was immediately drowned by a Yankee volley that hushed in death the voice of many a poor fellow. The Gen.[W. H. F. Lee], Dandridge,[23] Turner and myself were in the line and for a few minutes I began to think that Chancellorsville the Second had begun. Turner was struck in the shoulder at the first volley; he was just to my left and I saw him spin around in his saddle as the ball struck. The Yankees soon gave way and prisoners showed that we were not only fighting infantry, but that it was a large portion of the celebrated 2nd Corps, the crack corps of the Yankee Army. We nevertheless drove them upwards of two miles, killing and wounding 80 or 90, and capturing 98.[24]

Yesterday (Wednesday) was a comparatively quiet day, though considerable skirmishing was kept up throughout the day. I was engaged all day in ascertaining the localities of important by-roads and making a sketch of that everlasting Picket line. I really believe I spend half my time on the Picket line. You can imagine what a delightful time I have, nearly always in sight of the Yankees, and know but they may advance at any moment. Today (Thursday) we advanced again upon the enemy whom we found entrenched strongly just beyond an impassable swamp. After stirring them up considerably and drawing upon us several awful volleys, we found the position too strong and withdrew with but one man killed and several wounded. I think the attack will be renewed tomorrow.

Gen. Hampton is here and has lately been made successor to Gen. Stuart. Maj. Venable is now with him and Bob Lee and Turner both wounded reduces our staff considerably. Why can't I get a little furlough wound also?.... My accounts of the fighting must be very uninteresting to you, but we have nothing else to write about.

If I can get it, I will enclose a double photograph of The [Garnett] and myself taken in Richmond when last there. I attempted to color them but Capt. [Charles] Pierce[25] coming up to assist put out our eyes, which determined me to cut off my head except for the Zouave I have recently cultivated with so much pride. The above [sketch of sweeping mustache, the 'Zouave,' and goatee] is the style adopted by the entire staff and a handsome party we are as you may judge.

Tell Pa to look out for a horse for me. Kentucky falls down on every occasion. I am trying to trade him off. Any horse will do that is active. Where is my banjo?

It is strange, that of the few letters written by Frank Robertson during the last twenty months of the War that have been preserved, there are two long ones separated by only ten days. This one too is to his sister Kate and is dated August 28:

I have waited two days expecting to get a letter from home, but none having reached me as yet I presume they are all at HdQrs and will remain there until my return. Gen. [W. H. F.] Lee as you have already heard is my guest and with all due regard for his precious health, I would like his remaining so for at least a week longer,— alas! His head which three days ago was about the size of a half bushel, is fast assuming its natural dimensions, which even then compares to Tom Brender's as a mountain to a mouse. The swelling has unfortunately ceased,—he declares Richard is himself again and will return Tuesday to the Army. I have most earnestly cited several instances of relapse occurring from too early exposure of poison oak sufferers but it availith nothing,—and my arduous duties as ADC [Aide-de-Camp] on extra duty in Richmond are fast drawing to a close. I am however thankful for what I have had, and shall ever regard Poison Oak as a favorite plant. I have enjoyed my short stay exceedingly, the more so as I was considerably jaded down by the previous ten days of hard service, and was sorely in need of rest. I am thinner than I ever was before in good health,—weighing only 136 pounds, when it ought to be 150. I weighed yesterday at the boat, where I went to see Ella and Mary off. "Charly" was of course one of the party & says he has an indefinite furlough & can return to _____ [word illegible] when he pleases, which I presume will not be very shortly if we judge from the past.

Mary is looking very well & rather prettier than usual I think. She gave me a very cordial invitation to go up with them & I really felt almost tempted to run off for a few days—a week[']s quiet sojourn in the country would greatly benefit me I'm sure.

I called to see your friend Miss Lizzie Triplett yesterday and would really have scarcely known her, she has gained at least 30 pounds by her country visit and is really very pretty,—almost rivalling that independent young sister of hers, who by the way is becoming fast one of the belles of the City. I heard she had seven gentlemen to see her one evening alone.

I wish very much you were here to entertain our numerous lady visitors. Gen. Lee seems quite a favorite among them and several times there have been four or five in the parlor at a time. His oldest sister (Miss Mary Lee) comes in every day two or three times, and this morning came before breakfast and helped to discuss that meal with me. Comment is unnecessary. You may.

10 1/2 P.M. I was interrupted before I could finish the above sentence by the entrance of no other person than, Miss Mary Lee, escorted by the General. She seemed to feel very much at home and did not hesitate to say she had missed her supper. Being host and caterer, what could I do but offer food and comfort to my hungry guest and immediately stirred up Aunt Eleanor,[26] and greatly to her surprise, desired she should at once place before the young lady the best my house would afford which I regret to say consisted of stale bread (supply small), and very salty butter (half a pound on hand, and likely not to diminish much). She seemed to enjoy it however, and has just left escorted by Bob Lee, who also came in hungry. I like all the family I have seen, very much. They are very kind and unassuming and I expect you would like the girls if you knew them. I have never been introduced to the two younger ones,—they are still out of town.

Bob Lee got a letter from his father this evening. He sends a kiss to Mary Triplett through Bob who declares he is going over to deliver it tomorrow.

Ella sent you a good many messages, but I forget what they were— don't tell her. Mrs. Davenport has been very kind to me. She sent me an enormous watermellon & has kept me supplied with buttermilk. Sandford denies most positively being in love with Cousin Lettie. I think I saw Cousin Lou's friend, Capt. Stuart, in town today. It is rumored that commissioners are on the way south to negotiate an armistice. A right long letter to contain so little. Give my love to all & kiss Miss Alice, Cousin Lou & _____ [word illegible] for me. Bernard Taylor was killed last Sunday.

In his recollections Robertson elaborated on his experiences and duties during the Confederacy's last autumn:

My duties kept me on the picket line most of the time. On one occasion I was lying down drawing in a note book, the vedette looking on, when suddenly he cried, "Your horse is gone!" There, walking across the open field straight towards the Yankees was Miranda. I ordered the man to bring her back as he should have been holding her. Off he dashed and within probably not over fifty yards from the Yankee Vedette, he caught her and brought her back. I rather expected the Yank would fire on him, but he did not; at this period of the war, the outposts ceased annoying each other with useless firing. It never amounted to anything but constant annoyance and little execution. Outposts of an army are to watch each other, and only use their guns when an advance is made by either side. I was ashamed of my old warhorse for thus trying to desert to the enemy. I think she hoped to get full rations on the other side, for about this time both men and horses were slowly starving on the Confederate side.

That fall two North Carolinians (Tar heels we called them) were tried by court martial and ordered executed. Our whole division was ordered out to witness it. [Lt. Theodore S.] Garnett had to read the death warrant and I went to help him by holding his horse. Troops were drawn up on three sides of a square; two graves were dug and posts set up by them. The deserters were marched around the entire dismounted line of cavalry. Firing squads of twenty-four men faced the graves. The deserters were blindfolded and their arms tied behind them to the posts. Garnett read the death sentences. The squad officer raised his sword and, as it dropped, twenty-four men (Half with loaded muskets, but none knowing if his gun were loaded or blank) fired, and the two deserters hung dead to the posts. I had seen hangings, but this was my first sight of the firing squad in action. No doubt such things had to be, but it wasn't pleasant. One of the deserters was an unusually handsome young fellow, and he carried his overcoat on his arm as if hoping yet to need it. He had on a pair of home-knit gloves, and I couldn't help thinking that his mother had made them.

On November 2, 1864 Robertson wrote his mother from a camp sixteen miles southwest of Petersburg:

I have delayed writing longer than usual, but I know that you hear from me frequently through Kate & _____ [word illegible]. I wrote to Kate the day after reaching Camp, but have not yet gotten an answer. I suppose by this time they are at Mr. _____ [word illegible] again. Kate seemed very unwilling to return home again & was much relieved when she received permission thro' Cousin Eliza to stay.

The people of Richmond appear very confident of the security of the city and are all in much better spirits than when I left there to go home. The details were pouring in every day and the army rapidly filling up. All the detailed men in the many bomb-proof departments of the Army have also been put in the ranks. There has been quite a clearing out of them at our Hd Qrs and we are now reduced to four couriers instead of 12 or 14 as before. I look forward to a reduction of Staff Officers before the Winter is over, and I suppose in the Army slang I will be among the number "who go up to the front."

I find things at Hd Qrs much as I left them. My horses are looking in fine _____ [word illegible] and with the exception of an oil cloth & my trunk & paint box keys all my things are safe. All seemed glad to see me and the Gen. [W. H. F. Lee] promises me plenty of work with my pioneer party which he has recently permanently organized—it consists of 10 men from each regiment amounting in all to 70 mounted men—a very respectable body for a Second Lt. to command. The lines are quiet and there seems to be some probability of Grant changing his base for winter quarters. I think it unlikely however. Write and give me the Abingdon news. My best love to all.

Send my flannel drawers by the first opportunity—by some mistake or negligence they were left at home.

In another letter to his mother on November 28 Robertson reported just exactly what he was doing with his new command. He was at this time stationed in the vicinity of Monk's Neck along the Rowanty Creek.

My time is so closely occupied, dam making, forming abatis breastworks etc. with the Pioneer Corps as to prevent my writing as often as I would do. I ride down every morning directly after breakfast to this place, about four miles from camp, and usually do not get back to camp before sun down. I then discuss my dinner with no better relish I assure you, and candles only being issued to the Gen. and A.A.G. [Assistant Adjutant General] generally spend the few hours before bedtime in conversation with the "Subs," or playing on the banjo and guitar which The' Garnett has borrowed. I sent by Bob Lee today for a Confederate candle, which I hear are warranted to burn nine nights, besides being cheap. When it arrives I shall write more regularly.

We have been working at and about this dam for three weeks. Once it was finished, but unfortunately a heavy rain ensued immediately afterwards, breaking a dam above ours on Butler's picket line, and the stream thus reinforced made a breach in ours, undoing a weeks work in a couple of hours. The damage is now being repaired and the Gen. promises two days rest for our unavoidable Sunday's work.

By next Friday we hope to finish, tho' it is much more likely unless it rains, we shall have another sort of work on hand before that time.

The enemy are evidently bent on mischief. Both deserters and scouts report unusual activity and preparation in their camps. They shall find it a "hard road to travel" no matter where they make an advance. Our old A. N. Va. is in excellent condition and good spirits. It now numbers 40,000 muskets besides Cavalry and Artillery and can use up three times its numbers behind breastworks as it is.

The past two days have been delightful and remind me (as all the birds I imagine from the way they are singing) of the first warm days of Spring. We Sub's are very comfortably quartered now in Fly tents with chimneys (the latter our own make). I sleep pretty comfortably in spite of the cold nights we have recently had. Our beds are made of pinetwigs about six inches deep strewn between two large logs laid parallel & about three feet apart. Our overcoats are pillows & we lie on one blanket and cover with four.

The Gen. said today that Camp would be moved this week somewhere in the vicinity of Stony Creek Depot to be nearer supplies. I suppose we will then get wall tents and regular winter quarters be established.

I was sent to Petersburg last Monday and spent the night with Mr. Blackford. He was quite well and as snugly housed for the winter as its possible to be in canvass. He told me he expects Sister [Mary Robertson Blackford] to come soon and spend a few weeks, tho' I should certainly think it best she should wait until the fighting is over, and winter puts a stop to further movements.

When you come down, I want you should bring me something in the shape of eatables. Our mess is dead broke and we are living on bad beef _____ [word illegible] occasionally _____ [two words illegible] we can, _____ [word illegible] & a few spoiled potatoes. If you have any catsup to spare a bottle or two would be a great treat to us. A couple of bottles of brandy if Pa has any made would help us out amazingly about X-mas.

Tell Pa _____ [word illegible but is name of horse] leg is swollen tremendously & I am a little afraid will render her unserviceable. I did not ride her for a week and she is much better, but I am constantly afraid of a relapse. I think he had better have my other mare put in order or certainly not _____ [word illegible] to get _____ [word illegible].

Rheumatism is still troublesome, but I have not been knocked up one day with it _____ [word illegible] in the last two weeks. My best love to Pa, Sister & Wyndham.

In his recollections Robertson wrote more of his dam and what eventually happened to it:

I was ordered to build a military dam across a deep little river; it was to be the last of a series of dams made as a line of defence from Petersburg south. The order provided for a roadway along the top. My pioneers, one hundred picked mechanics from cavalry ranks and also one regiment of cavalry, were ordered to report at the dam site the next day as a combined working force. I was somewhat rattled over the job. The Colonel of the North Carolina regiment sent me was a whole-souled old fellow, and he stood by me manfully on the job. It was quickly completed with so many workers, and cavalry pickets were at once riding over its head. We had no tools except axes, shovels and picks. I sent out to "press" a cart without success. A Tarheel officer offered to make a wheel barrow—wheels of bumwood sawed from a tree of the right diameter, and the rest of these wonders made of seven slabs of oak on the clapboard order. Having no grease, each barrow screeched on a different key and greatly amused the workers. A short time after the completion of what the men termed "Robertson's Dam Dam," heavy rains flooded the country and "Robertson's Dam Dam" busted, as did all the others. This consoled me, but never during my army life was I so "conflushcated" as when that order was given me.

The winter evidently was hard on Robertson's health for he was forced to seek refuge in Richmond either sometime in December or early January. A letter written to him on January 8 by his close friend The' Garnett informed him of camp doings and urged him to get better and return as soon as possible:

Dear Frank,

As Phil Dandridge starts to Richmond in the morning, I take occasion to drop you a line. I must apologize for not spending the last night I was in town with you. I had to make such an early start Saturday morning and I was up so late Friday night that I thought it best not to disturb you. I had a miserable trip back to camp arriving here last Monday evening—two days over my leave. I had to make a written apology to Genl. Robt E. [Lee] for having overstayed my time. I haven't heard from it yet, but I suppose I'll be CtMartialed and shot.

There is nothing new or interesting in this quarter of the globe. We are still camped near Bellefield [Belfield] tho' there are daily rumors of our moving. I think it probable that we will remain here some weeks yet. We have a comparatively dull time of it here, tho' preparations are on foot for making it somewhat less so. [Maj. Gen. Matthew C.] Butler's[27] Division is going to give a Ball. A very heavy thing I reckon it will be.

Genl. W.H.F. [Lee] gave a grand dinner here last Wednesday. It was really a splendid dinner—as good as could be gotten up. The Comdg officer of each regt in our Divn and Genl's Butler, Barringer and Col. [Richard L. T.] Bèale[28] with their A.A.Gs. [assistant adjutant general] and a few other officers were present. Genl. Hampton was invited but did not attend. [Maj. George] Freaner[29] however came over and ate for him. I couldn't begin to tell you what was on the table, but I'll just name a few articles: Mutton, beef, ham and cabbage, oysters fried, oysters stewed, sausage and vegetables till you couldn't rest. Dessert: Ice-cream and cake, apples etc Eggnog, apple-toddy and new—[word unknown] circulated more freely than I have seen anywhere since the war began. But enough of this—

Your horses are looking very well. Your mare was lame a short time ago but has gotten over it. We are getting 10 lbs of corn and plenty of long forage. Sam is anxiously awaiting his relief to come. If you want your horses sent to you let me know. If you could draw forage for them in Richmond you could have a good time there this winter. But when do you expect to return to camp? I wish you would make haste and get well. Bob Lee and I are the sole representatives of the "Hill-mess." We get full rations of course.

Write to me and let me know how you are getting along.

Present my kindest regards to your sisters, remember me to your Cousin Lou and believe me, very truly yr. friend

T.S.G. Jr.

P.S. Bob Lee is caterer, and as such requests the sum of $16.00 (sixteen dollars) from you to settle your account for December.

Yours The

Despite Garnett's urging, Robertson did not return to duty until sometime in February or March. When he finally rejoined his companions his duties once again put him in danger:

As I have mentioned, my duties kept me constantly on the picket line. On one occasion I passed the picket in a deep wood and rode out to the vedette line, half a mile beyond. All seemed quiet. I returned to the picket (some ten or twelve men) and was talking to them when a volley was fired into us from the deep wood around. I saw the young man who was sitting on his horse talking to me fall backwards just as a bullet scattered bark from a tree near us and stung my face. I stood not upon the order of my going, but went. As I reached the road, I encountered a dozen or so Yanks riding full speed my way. Such a yelling and shooting, but Miranda and rider again went closely pursued. A dead horse lay in the road, and there and then would have occurred my downfall but for a gap in the fence: Miranda's aversion to a dead horse was her worst fault and it never abated in spite of daily experience.

When I reached the dam, General Rooney Lee was there. My report of the sudden ambush sent me off full tilt to mount the division. I rode from regiment to regiment giving the order, and the division was soon mounted and ready for action. The Yanks however seemed content with capturing our vedette and picket. I never knew what damage was done by the ambush, but apparently I was the only one who escaped, as the squad I met in the road showed the Yanks had gotten behind our outpost line. Here again Miranda's speed saved me.

There were fights and skirmishes more or less serious most every day after this until the breaking of our lines at the Battle of Five Forks.

The first day of April 1865 marked the beginning of the last act of the tragedy. General Lee had learned that General Grant, continuing his shift to the left in efforts to turn the Confederate right flank, was sending Sheridan due west to Dinwiddie Court House; then Sheridan was to turn north, through a lonely crossroads known as Five Forks, to cut the South Side Rail Road. Such an interruption of this important traffic artery would compel the evacuation of Petersburg, and thus, indirectly, of Richmond. Lee did not have enough men to extend his right in strength, so he ordered Fitz Lee to bring Munford and his 1800 troopers south, across the James. When Fitz Lee reported to Petersburg, he was finally placed in command of the cavalry corps, and he was ordered to Five Forks. Rooney Lee and his 2400 cavalrymen were called in from Stony Creek forty miles away, and Maj. Gen. Thomas Rosser[30] brought over his 1200 men who had been fighting in the Valley. Maj. Gen. George E. Pickett and about five thousand of his foot-soldiers were also assembled by March 30.

On the extreme right of the Confederate front that day, along the White Oak Road which ran from east to west through Five Forks, was Major General Rooney Lee; west of the road junction was Col. Thomas T. Munford.

The story goes that Rosser had seized some very fine shad the day before and, knowing that hunger was not confined to the lowly conscripts, he invited General Fitz Lee and General Pickett to a "shad-bake" on All Fools' Day. On the day before these gentlemen had driven Sheridan back to Dinwiddie Court House without difficulty and were not expecting him to be heavily reinforced over night. So the senior cavalry officer and the senior infantry officer in the vicinity hastened with light hearts to eat shad with their friend a short distance north of the crossroads. Neither had thought it worth while to place some one else in charge, or even to say where he might be found if needed.

Robertson recorded the sad events of Five Forks in his memoirs:

We were camped at Five Forks when the Yanks advanced. The Gilliams lived on a part of the battlefield, and Miss Bena Gilliam[31] was quite a belle and much admired by General Rooney Lee and his staff. A heavy skirmish preceded the battle. I was sent to see how things were progressing. When I came back to report, General Lee was talking to Miss Bena,—no staff or couriers visible. I was immediately sent back to observe the skirmish again; found our lines outnumbered, flanked and falling back. I reported at once to General Lee at the same place with the same company. I was immediately sent to fetch the Headquarters ambulance which promptly arrived, and Miss Bena mounted it with bag and baggage and drove off. There and then I saw all my worldly possessions depart from me forever; nice uniform, only used when I went home to Richmond, a roll of four splendid red blankets gathered on the battlefield, paint box and many maps and instruments for map-making, beautiful chased English sabre, etc. Bullets were flying when our big ambulance and four mules dashed off. I have often wondered where the General's staff and couriers were during this escape of Miss Bena.

I carried a message to General Pickett to tell him our cavalry line was being flanked. I met him riding full speed up the road and, before I could say a word, he called out to me, "Don't talk to me. My lines are broken." I didn't talk, but rode full tilt to General Lee and reported the interview.

I saw a long line of Yankee cavalry advancing in line of battle, two small regiments of ours facing them. The General told me to order these regiments to charge. Then came a general melee and mix-up, with Pickett's men retreating in confusion behind us. I hardly know how to describe things just here, yet the fact remains we were greatly outnumbered and in retreat. I was lost from my General and staff, and found myself after dark with Colonel Moon's North Carolina regiment of our division.[32] I shall never forget the blare of the Yankee bugles blowing the charge, and the deep voice of Colonel Moon, "Form a line, men, form a line." The crashing oncome of the Yankee cavalry through the dark woods, the feeble fire of Colonel Moon's men and then the hasty retreat. This seemed to go on for an hour or so.

The Yankees reported the capture of 3,244 men and four guns, and General R. E. Lee's right flank was shattered. The second night after Five Forks he would cross the Appomattox River in retreat. That day, however, Rooney Lee managed to elude the Federal forces and join with Fitz Lee north of Hatcher's Run. The real cause of this disaster to the Confederates was that Sheridan's well-fed troopers, equipped with repeating carbines, supported by Warren's Fifth Corps and other troops, numbered 53,740 against hardly 10,000 Rebels.

The final few days were sadly recalled by Robertson years later:

At last towards daybreak I found General Rooney Lee. He sent me to General Fitz Lee to report and get information generally. I found Fitz Lee some miles away and he told me Richmond had fallen and our army was in full retreat towards Lynchburg. I carried this sad news to General Rooney Lee. We skirmished and retreated all day. We stopped at a farm house—staff assessed to pay for supper. My last $10.00 Confederate note was swiped, we had not fed since the day before, so I didn't begrudge my last X. Retreat resumed and continued for a week. Skirmishes and starvation, abandonment of trains, general and hopeless distress and suffering. It seemed we would perish for drinking water, though starvation was uncomfortable and dreams of feasting stayed with us night and day.

I was ordered one day to take my pioneers, reduced to perhaps a dozen out of the original hundred, and destroy a bridge "as soon as the rear guard has passed." I dismounted four good axe-men and each was to cut a stringer as rapidly as possible when the flying rearguard had passed. This was not a job to delight anyone,—but here came the rear guard, and close behind a cloud of Yanks. As soon as our men cleared the bridge, our four axes attacked the stringers. Our mounted pioneers and some men on a hill behind us held the pursuit in check and down came the bridge,—and off we went under heavy fire. I did not see any of those near me fall, though several horses did.

I met George Peterkin, an old school mate in Richmond and afterwards Bishop of West Virginia.[33] He told me where there was a pen of corn hidden in the woods. This was my third day of total abstinence from food of any kind and very little water, for lack of which I suffered most. My canteen had gone with the ambulance. Thompson,[34] one of General Stuart's old couriers, had been with me since the day before, and we found the corn and ate it ravenously. He told me he was to be married as soon as the war was over, and he raved over the beauty and attractions of the girl. We slept by a straw rick. Infantry arrived during the night, removed every particle of straw rick, stole my overcoat and stole oats from my horse, and were a general nuisance. Thompson was killed shortly after we resumed our march the next morning. Several other good friends of mine were killed in this retreat, including Robert H. Goldsborough, who had been captured at Brandy Station and had just been exchanged.

At the High Bridge my camp boy Bob rode into where we were lying in the woods. It was the first time I had seen him since we left Petersburg. I told him to shift saddles, give me Lily and take Miranda. He put both saddles on the ground,—just then some shells entered the woods; he put his saddle back on Lily and departed, leaving me my saddle and Miranda.[35] I didn't see him again until I reached Abingdon. He stayed with me—faithful and attentive—until I went to Richmond with my father some weeks afterwards. Bob disappeared the next day and we have never heard of him since. He belonged in eastern Virginia and I suppose he went back there. Bob was my third camp boy, Sam, Ben and Bob,— all were sincerely devoted to me, I am sure. Sam belonged to me, my only slave. I offered him his freedom several times, explained that all that was necessary to do was to wave my handkerchief, ride up and deliver him to a Yank picket, and the thing was done. He showed no disposition to adopt my plan, however, and seemed as averse to capture as I was myself.

The retreat from Petersburg was a great trial to the Army of Northern Virginia. Frazzled and famished, these unconquered soldiers went down and out with defiance on every brow and sorrow in every heart. General Grant appeared to appreciate conditions, in strong contrast to Sheridan, Custer and some other U.S. leaders, and his kind treatment at Appomattox was and is greatly appreciated.

Very early in the morning of April 9, 1865, a last stand of Lee's ragged remnant seemed arranged for, and skirmishers and battle line went forward and drove back the enemy, capturing three guns[36] and some prisoners. It looked like old times. Our division connected with the infantry's right of the Second Corps under Major General John B. Gordon, and just at the point of juncture the guns were captured. To our right was Rosser's division and then Munford's.

The infantry line was still advancing and firing. I was sitting my horse by General Rooney Lee when one of the batteries opened upon what looked like a charging regiment of the enemy's infantry. I saw in a moment that they were prisoners being driven towards us by a few of our cavalry, and called the General's attention to it. He sent me at once to stop the battery's fire. Shortly after we came across several pieces of artillery our cavalry had just captured and to our left I noticed the infantry battle line advancing with the skirmishers actively firing on the retreating Yankees.

Just here came the surprise of my life as a soldier; to my astonishment, General Rooney Lee ordered me to ride the infantry line and order them to "cease firing and fall back." I carried this message of great import until I met an infantry staff officer carrying the same order.[37]

I returned to General Rooney Lee and then learned that our army was surrendered and the four years' struggle was at an end. This seemed incredible in spite of the fact we were a forlorn hope worn to a frazzle.

As we were riding back, I visited a wounded Yank I had previously passed. He was an officer of high rank, I judged from his overcoat and equipment. I saw he was dying and took his overcoat as I had none. A heavy gold chain was in evidence and there were doubtless greenbacks in his pockets, but I could never "go through" a man, either a dead one or a prisoner. He tried to tell me something most painfully while I was getting his overcoat from under him, but I didn't feel I had time to hear it. Passing that way afterwards, I found him dead, and his gold watch and chain missing. That Yankee overcoat was a grand affair and gave me comfort for several years, though of course I had it dyed.

We had been moving slowly back towards Appomattox for half a mile or more when General Lee called me, saying, "I don't know where General Fitz Lee (commanding all the cavalry) is, and must assume command, so go rapidly, find General Rosser and tell him his and Munford's divisions are included in the terms of the surrender, and to report with them."

After a few miles hard ride towards Lynchburg, I caught up with General Rosser and delivered the order. He promptly ordered me to go back and tell General Lee, "not your General Lee, but General R. E. Lee, that I am going to attack Grant's wagon train in rear." I didn't want to go back, and he should have sent one of his own staff besides. I saw Colonel Chew[38] of the Horse Artillery, whom I knew well, and he agreed with me. General Rosser noted conditions and, calling me to him, said, "I will be greatly obliged if you will take this message as you know where to find General R. E. Lee (which I didn't), and I'll send a man with you." When he looked back on the column of cavalry for "a man," it was interesting to note how they all avoided his eyes. However, he ordered out old Bushy Whiskers, as I dubbed him, and he and I started on our mission, very unwillingly heading back to Appomattox, while General Rosser and his two brigades of cavalry proceeded towards Lynchburg. Rosser's plan to attack Grant's wagon train in the rear didn't appear reasonable to me and was, as I surmised, never attempted.

We butt[ed] into several Yankee pickets and, not knowing how we might be treated, took to the woods promptly. We met Curtis,[39] General Rooney's scout. He wore a coat, blue on one side and grey on the other, and, showing the blue, was a frequent visitor to Yankee camps, and a most valuable and daring scout. Curtis, learning the situation, offered to carry my message, as he "wished to go back to our men anyway." So I wrote the message and he went back with it. I have never heard of him since, and have wondered if his turn-coat had been discovered and he had been summarily dealt with.

Bushy and I then determined to look for the James River and get away from the mess on this the south side. In our march we encountered a deserted Confederate wagon train in the road, no teams or men visible. We dismounted and began to kick open a couple of officers' hand trunks for the laudable purpose of covering our nakedness. Just as mine flew open—displaying a full assortment of just what I needed—I heard several shots and, looking under the wagon, saw a column of Yankee cavalry coming at a trot, calling as they came to "surrender." I was next to the woods and made good my escape, but Bushy was on the road side and I'm sure they took him in. Why they did not shoot me is a surprise to me until this day.

I now felt like the last of the Mohicans, alone absolutely in an unknown forest and I had not the slightest idea of the points of the compass. I knew the James River was north from Appomattox, but which way was north? After an hour or so of hopeless wandering, I saw an artilleryman with his red trimmings galloping through the woods. I called and asked him where he was going.

"To General Lee's Army."

"General Lee's Army has surrendered."

"You're a damned liar!"

"Go on and find out for yourself, damn you!"

His gentle remark to me was irritating, though I admitted the feeling that prompted it. He turned his horse, galloped up, touched his hat,

"Beg your pardon, I just can't credit it."

It really seemed incredible that our grand old army had actually surrendered. I imagine such a contingency had never been dreamed of by 90 per cent of its soldiers. I assured my new found friend, Leigh, from Charleston, S.C., that it was a melancholy fact, and asked him if he knew the way to the James River. He had just come from there, he had been engaged in "burying artillery." I found he had been riding on a narrow road through the woods that led directly to the river, which I had been heading for unknowingly. We rode back to the James and found a number of men crossing, some in small boats, leading their swimming horses. Leigh paid our passage on a flatboat navigated by two negroes who charged $1.00 Confederate per head,—I hadn't a cent.

We went up the north bank, recrossed by ferry to Mt. Athos, the home of my uncle, Judge John Robertson. I ate a ton of biscuits and we went to sleep under a cedar tree in the garden. Cousin Powhatan waked us about midnight. He told us we better go, as the Yanks had just burned the bridge across the river and were likely to appear at Mt. Athos any time. We rolled out, led our horses down the mountain, roused the lock-keeper and told him my uncle wanted him to ferry us across the river again.

We reached Lynchburg about 4 a.m. Rabble shouting, "Hurrah, hurrah for the Union!" Leigh stopped there, but I rode on alone, headed for the Meadows, two hundred miles west. I saw, or rather could hear, cavalry in front. I heard someone say something about Henry Lee.[40] I yelled, "Henry Lee!" and rode up to a man who was waiting for me, who remarked, "Did you call me, General Rosser?" I informed him who I was, and that my division of cavalry had surrendered, and that I was lonesome and far from home. He said General Munford and some of his staff were right ahead and to come join them. General Munford I knew well; he was also from Richmond, and our families were intimate. He took me up to his farm some fourteen miles from Lynchburg, where I feasted and slept the sleep of the weary for nearly twenty-four hours straight.

We left there about 10 a.m. on the 11th, passing through Liberty now known as Bedford, to spend the night at Captain McDaniel's. He gave us whisky and honey before breakfast the next morning,—a decided hit.[41] We traveled about 25 miles and stopped at Mr. Riddle's on top of the Blue Ridge about four miles from Big Lick now called Roanoke, plenty of forage and grass, so Henry Lee and I concluded to remain at Riddle's till General Munford left for Danville. On Friday, the 14th, I paid a visit to Mr. Taylor's,—found a child sick and so I could not see the ladies. I saw one of General Lee's couriers who gave me an account of the surrender and furnished me with the order of General Lee.

The next day, leaving Henry Lee at Gish's mill to wait for General Munford, I started for home one hundred and fifty miles away.[42] I had not a cent of money, and the people all along the way had been absolutely stripped of food by the soldiers going home from Lee's Army. I had filled one side of my saddle pockets with coffee from a burning wagon on retreat, and this was a godsend, for most of the farm ladies were glad to give me a few bites for a handful of coffee. Sleeping along the road in patches of woods and in fence corners, and acquiring horse feed in the darksome night where I could find it, I reached Newbern, where Mr. Jordan, an old acquaintance known in Abingdon, fed me up and gave me a half bushel of corn to sustain Miranda, who was barely able to sustain her own light weight, let alone my hundred and thirty pounds. [Robertson later stated that when they left Henry Lee he noticed that Miranda was pretty well exhausted and put her head over his shoulder to help her along to home. He commented that, "It was my turn."] I reached Seven Mile Ford and breakfasted quite heartily with my cousins, the John M. Prestons. Charley Preston rode to Abingdon with me.

As I approached Chilhowie, I saw what seemed to be about twenty-five or more Yankee cavalry. They were down near where the railroad crossed the Middle Fork of the Holston. Just then a train going west appeared, two flats covered with men standing without any cover. The blue coats halted the train and the homeseeking Confederates, unarmed and ragged, were made to dismount from the flats, and I heard afterwards were all robbed of what little they possessed. The train was then started: it ran out on the bridge and I saw the entire outfit go down through the prepared cut stringers into the river, thus depriving these poor soldiers of a much needed help in reaching their distant homes.

On seeing me two men dashed up in front of me, and sat facing each other on opposite sides of the road. Charley Preston had stopped at his farm on the road and would catch up with me. I did not like the looks of these blue-clad men and supposed them Yankees, but I made up my mind that somebody would get hurt if they attempted to take my horse, as I had heard along the road was quite in fashion by roving bands of nobodies. I stopped near them, hoping Charlie would join me. I said,"Good morning, gentlemen."

No response. I then asked wasn't there an accident to that train, and was anybody hurt.

"Yes," (with an oath) "A lot of men killed. Where are you from?"

"General Lee's Army."

"Where are you going?"

"Home to Abingdon."

Just then I heard Charley coming. I pulled out my pistol and, as he rode alongside, we together passed between the brutes. My pistol seemed to surprise and mortify them. There were no further remarks from them and we came safely home. Why they did not all hands come in pursuit I don't know, but I believe they had a cowardly fear of some of them getting hurt. The courage of that class of scoundrels is only high when there is no possibility of resistance.

This same gang had robbed seven men in sight of Abingdon. They were under command of a parolee named Champ Ferguson, who claimed to be a Confederate whose family had been horribly ill-treated by the Yanks, whom he slaughtered without mercy when any fell into his hands. He was hanged by the Yanks after the war, I've heard.[43]

We reached the Meadows about half past five, Monday p.m., April 18. The family was all out on the front porch and they were surprised when I rode up as Bob had arrived the day before and he swore that he knew I was captured. I believe now, as always, that our cause was just, and our action inevitable, patriotic and justifiable; and I assert and swear "by Granny" I'd do the same again under the same conditions.

The end had come and with it a sort of compensating relief that the wretched killing was over, that men might feel that death and suffering were not forever staring them in the face, for we had begun to know that it was only a matter of time when the soldier who did his duty would meet his end. This became the settled conviction of the veteran. Though the end of the war was some consolation at least, the utter depression following Lee's surrender was infinite. It seemed beyond belief that his ever-victorious army should suffer such humiliation. No feeling of disgrace attached to it, for the humblest soldier felt and knew that it was no fault of General Lee or his men that brought it about, but overwhelming well-fed numbers against an exhausted, starved-out remnant.

The failure to create a Southern Confederacy did not especially concern us. The freeing of the slaves I would have approved had it not been done so brutally, almost inviting the massacre of the unprotected families of absent men. Virginia as a rule did not approve of slavery, and its perpetuation had virtually nothing to do with her heroic fight against the U. S. Government, which so foolishly forced her into this war in which she became the mainstay and bulwark, as well as sufferer. When she flies a defiant flag, right or wrong, her sons will stand behind it. I have no regrets over her action in 1861. She and any other people of high-spirited independence would do the same under similar circumstances.

I cannot close these memoirs without paying tribute to my old home, Richmond. She was the Thermopylae of the South. Her gates were passed after four years' defense, but she enacted an enormous toll for it. Her young men without exception offered their services to Virginia and gave an unprecedented number of their lives for her.

Robertson received his parole on May 22, 1865 as a first lieutenant[44] of engineers and staff officer to W.H.F. Lee. On the 25th of the same month he took the oath as was required. There was, however, one other bit of business that the U.S. government had with the ex-Confederate engineer as the following document shows.

> Office Provost Marshal Sub Dist. of Holston
> Abingdon Sep 14 1865

> This is to certify that F.S. Robertson of Washington County— Va. has permission to retain in his possession one (1) Gov't Saddle which he promises to care for and return to the U.S. Government on the 1st day of January 1866 or pay a fair valuation price for same.

Whether the saddle was a "souvenir" from the war or was just being borrowed is unclear. Neither is there a record of whether Robertson kept the saddle or paid for it. In any event the war was over and Robertson looked to the future.

8

After the War

Captain Frank Robertson was more fortunate than many Confederate veterans. He had never been wounded; he had never been a prisoner of war; he was able to return to the farm where he had grown up; and his old home, The Meadows, though in territory held by the enemy for several weeks, had not been burnt to the ground. Yet great changes had taken place. At twenty-four Robertson was no longer the carefree, beloved son of wealthy parents who had plenty of slaves to do everything that had to be done. No longer was he a boy who had never shouldered responsibility greater than that of planning a dance or getting up a deer hunt. The regime in which he had been brought up, the way of life he loved, was a thing of the past.

Many of the friends of his youth had been killed. Others had been gravely wounded, with the loss of an arm or a leg perhaps. The most unfortunate ones suffered a crushed spirit. The Army of Northern Virginia had been something like a big fraternity. A fellow was always running into kinsman and lifelong friends, and their friends. They fought an almost intimate war. A soldier might learn that an old school mate he had been talking with the night before had been killed, or see his first cousin's head blown off. No young man can return from four years of fighting quite the same man he was before.

After a brief trip to Richmond with his father, Robertson wasted no time in idle repining. Despite his poor health, he pitched in and tried to make The Meadows once again a paying proposition, though with hired hands. Wyndham Robertson, now in his sixties, considered himself an old man (though he was to live more than a score of years), and he was perfectly willing to let the returned soldier run the farm. Indeed he expected it of him.

From The Meadows on October 19, 1865, Robertson wrote to his father in Richmond to advise him of what was happening at home:

> Farming operations are progressing quite satisfactorily. The hands that do work are working well, but not commencing as early in the day as they should. Tho' much better, I am still unwell, or I should attend more closely to such matters. I have employed Sam to take charge of the Stable. He left Blackwell, as he says, because his wife wished to go back to Mr. Floyd, now living in town. I give him till 9 o'clock to finish with the horses, and then put him at anything I may desire until sundown. He is doing admirably so far and is decidedly improved by his visit to Blackwell. John, whom he succeeded at the stable, I have retained as a field hand....
>
> The sorrel colts I have stabled, but have only broken one as yet. There seems to be no demand for horses in this country, and I see no prospect of selling....
>
> It seems that the house you bought of Vance belonged to the U. S. Government and is of course public property. Patton saw the Freedman's Agent in regard of it and was informed it belonged to the U. S. Gov., the greater part having been built for a stable by the Confederate States....
>
> I heard yesterday, the troops in town were to leave tomorrow, to be succeeded by an infantry regiment. Please bring me a couple of heavy undershirts—I lost mine in the retreat.

About a month later Robertson wrote to his sister, Kate. He described some of what was and was not going on in and around The Meadows:

> Abingdon is full of girls, but decidedly stupid, no parties, no dances, dinners, nothing going on but a little promenading in the evening.... I have been visiting very little. I am of course frequently at the Johnstons and a few days since drove Cousin Lou[1] and Lettie up to the Saltworks on a shopping expedition, of which I suppose Cousin Lou has by this time informed you. They pitched in with a vim and bought about half the poor man had, which made me feel so poor, that I became indignant—pitched in myself and bought 50 dollars worth, more than I had funds to pay for. Among other things some red flannel undershirts, that have nearly scratched the life out of me and to which you must attribute my bad writing.

Ma is slowly improving, but still confined to her bed and suffers from having to lie so long in the same position.... Sister [Mary—Mrs. W. W. Blackford] is now staying regularly up here to attend to Ma.

Three months after that letter Mary Robertson Blackford died in childbirth at the birth of her seventh child. Following the death of his wife, Colonel Blackford left for Louisiana. Governor Robertson wanted him to develop a plantation he was planning to leave to his daughter's surviving children (three had died as babies). After Blackford had worked hard for several years, a Mississippi flood washed away everything he had done. The Colonel in his discouragement was quite willing to turn over to his young brother-in-law full responsibility for bringing up his children. When other members of the clan waxed critical of this arrangement, all they could get out of Frank Robertson was, "Colonel Blackford was a magnificent soldier." As for the children, though they always called him "Uncle Frank," they loved him like a father and talked about him with affection all their lives.

In 1867 Robertson went north to visit his first cousin, Eliza Skipwith Gordon, in Baltimore as he had been planning to do for several years. As he was leaving their house to come home, he ran into beautiful Miss Stella Wheeler, whose sister, Mary, had married Eliza Gordon's son. On his part, it was love at first sight, and he changed his plans quickly. However, she refused to be swept off her feet. She had been raised in a convent, where she had learned to play the piano, but it would appear that she did not think this the ideal training for a farmer's wife.

Finally she consented to marry him if he would promise never to ask her to do any work. Though doubtless there were many in Abingdon who wondered what put it into the young man's head to propose to this girl who had not even been born in Virginia when there were so many Virginia girls looking for husbands, Robertson knew what he wanted, and he promised. They were married January 30, 1868, less than three months after they met. The old soldier always kept his word, and she devoted four hours a day to reading her Bible.

The Captain's bride hailed from Rockville, Maryland. She had never been south of the Potomac River at the time of her marriage; probably she had never been seventy-five miles from the scene of her birth. Certainly she had never lived on a farm. The contrast between life in the Baltimore convent and life on the farm in the Virginia mountains must have seemed pretty tremendous to her, but if she ever regretted her bargain she never told anyone.

It would be hard to imagine two people more unlike than Captain Robertson and his wife. Fearless and unconventional, lusty and generous was he, all full of fun, but the word that best describes him is "warm." That word could never be used in speaking of her. Reserved, dignified, sensitive and considerate are suitable terms to describe her. A grande dame to her fingertips, even in her old age she was beautiful as a queen. Their dissimilarities, which certainly grew no less pronounced in the more than fifty-eight years they lived together with rarely a night under separate roofs, seemed rather to make them more devoted to each other.

Robertson's first child was Marie, born on October 24, 1868. She married Willoughby Reade, head of the English Department at Episcopal High School, and for twenty-two years she shared his life at the school. During that time Frank Robertson Reade and three other younger daughters put in their appearances.

Marie Reade had a lot of pride. She was very proud of her husband and his success in teaching. But teachers were not well paid, and the family had to be fed through the summer. In 1901 she decided to open a camp for girls, the very first to be started in the United States, at The Meadows. She hoped in this way to pay her family's expenses for the summer, and eventually did better than that.

That first summer she had tents pitched on the lawn for the campers. The girls played tennis in dresses to their ankles and, weather permitting, at 5 o'clock tea was served on the grass courts. Horsemanship, however, was the great attraction. Because it was safer the girls were allowed to ride in divided skirts, and this was considered rather daring in the early 1900s. Frank Robertson was always interested in the camp, and in the first dozen years he would often accompany the girls on their rides, offering them pointers on how to sit their horses.

Among the horses the girls rode were some descendants of Miranda, Robertson's old war horse. In the 1880s the grand old mare had gone blind. One day she found her way up the hill into the backyard where her master was. She was very old, and she was suffering. No one else had loved her as Robertson had; no one else should give her rest. So he went into the house for his Winchester. Years later he related that he would rather have shot anyone else in the family.

Eventually the camp grew too large for The Meadows, so Robertson gave his daughter a tract of land a mile away where there was more room. Here permanent buildings were erected, as well as substantial frames and floors for tents. One of the cottages was called the Captain's cabin, and sometimes he slept there. The girls loved to have him come over to supper, and afterwards around the campfire tell them tales and sing to them the old songs with his banjo.

Over the years Captain Robertson had become one of the best known citizens of Washington County and had lent his support to maintaining law and order ever since the unsettled days just after the War. He let it be known that he regarded his daughter's campers as his own granddaughters. As a result the girls could go anywhere in the county at any hour of the day or night, alone or in groups, perfectly protected by the old veteran's stern reputation.

Even before The Meadows became the scene of the girls' camp it held yearly gatherings of a different sort. Shortly after the war Robertson began treating the Confederate veterans of his neighborhood, especially those of Co. I, 48th Virginia Infantry, to a summer picnic at The Meadows. A grand time was had by all, and many of Robertson's grandchildren remembered the days of those outdoor barbecues with fondness. There is no record as to what extent Robertson became involved with the numerous Confederate Veteran camps that sprang up across the country in the 1900s, but on May 30, 1907, the old engineer was present at the Confederate reunion in Richmond for a special event.

After years of planning and fund raising, the old veterans of Lee's Cavalry Corps came together to unveil a statue of their beloved leader, General Stuart. Among those attending were some of Stuart's staff, now wearing gray of a different sort. Chiswell Dabney and Robertson rode to the ceremony in the same carriage, and at first, had great difficulty recognizing each other. Both hoped that their fellow passenger and former staff officer, Walter Hullihen, "Honey-bun" to Stuart, now an Episcopal minister, would keep his opening prayer short to spare the legs of the old vets. Hullihen prayed—long and hard—and The' Garnett, Robertson's old friend, gave the address which few heard over the crowd noise. In the end they parted. It is not known if they ever saw each other again. Time was taking its toll.

Time, too, was growing short for the former assistant engineer. Throughout the early months of 1926, he complained of being weak and feeling "no-'count" and was coughing a great deal which caused

soreness in his throat. He said that it wasn't any fun to live a long
time after all your friends were dead.

On August 10, 1926, the old soldier suddenly rose from his bed
about midnight and walked to the window. And then, a cancer
having eroded into the great artery of his neck, he sank down quietly and was soon gone as peacefully as his friend Channing Price
had gone at Chancellorsville.

Robertson's grandson, Frank Robertson Reade, tells best what
remains of the story:

> All the necessary arrangements for my grandfather's funeral had
> been made when I got home the next day, but my Aunt Katy was
> concerned that she had not been able to find his cherished letter from
> General Stuart anywhere in the Captain's office. A week or so before,
> she told me, he had laughingly said that he would like to have this
> letter tucked in with him when the end came. I knew that he had
> wrapped the letter in an old newspaper and had hidden it on the top
> shelf of his desk.
>
> I went into his office and got the letter:

Hd. Qrs. Cavalry Corps
Sept. 21st, 1863.

Dear Lieutenant:

> I deeply regret the continuance of your illness, for I had hoped by
> this time you would be able to join us. I know very well that you
> could not be kept from your post except by inexorable necessity. It
> needed no surgeon's certificate to satisfy me of it.
>
> I am glad of the present opportunity of expressing to you my sense
> of the usefulness, the bravery, the devotion to duty and daring for
> which you were distinguished during your stay with me. I sent you
> through fiery ordeals at Chancellorsville and elsewhere from which I
> scarcely hoped to see you return, but rejoiced to see you escape. You
> will never forget those trials and I hope the kind Providence which so
> signally favored you will soon see you restored to the field and to
> your much attached comrades.
>
> Present my kindest regards to your father's family and believe me

Your sincere friend,
J. E. B. Stuart
Major General.

> For a long time I looked at this letter after I had copied it. Then
> I went into the room where the old soldier lay, and tucked it in with
> him. And, as I looked at him for the last time, I knew that, from his
> whole eighty-five years of life, there was nothing that my grandfa-
> ther would rather have taken with him than that letter from his com-
> rade and commander.

Notes

Introduction

1. The deed to the Meadows is dated May 8, 1823, from James Bradley, Jr. and wife to Francis Smith. Francis was also the true name of Frank Smith Robertson although he never used it.

2. James Coleman Motley was born at "The Meadows," Washington County, Virginia, in 1920. As a little boy he would sit by the hour at his grandfather's feet, listening in rapt silence to the old soldier's stories. When the boy grew up he followed in the footsteps of his grandfather to the University of Virginia. While there, with good use of his summers, he earned his commission in the Marine Corps and, when his country needed him, he too left the university, ready to fight.

   Captain Robertson's heart was ever young, and he could have understood what was in the heart of the young Marine when he fought at Guadalcanal; when he led his company through eight hundred yards of surf at Tarawa; when he was shot down over Tinian in 1944. But the old veteran would have regretted that his grandson never had the privilege of fighting on a spirited mount like Miranda.

Chapter 1

1. Wyndham Robertson (June 26, 1803-February 11, 1888) was the twenty-seventh governor of the State of Virginia. If not one of the oldest citizens, he was certainly one of the "most respectable citizens" of the State at that time of his governorship. Three years after his term expired, he had retired from public life to raise thoroughbreds on his farm in the southwest corner of Virginia.

2. J.E.B. Stuart to his mother, January 31, 1860. Adele H. Mitchell, ed. *The Letters of Major General James E. B. Stuart* (Stuart-Mosby Historical Society, 1990) 184-190. [Ed.]

3. Henry Alexander Wise (December 3, 1806-September 12, 1876) had been a lawyer but became involved in politics taking a strong pro-Southern position on states' rights and slavery. He served in the U.S. House of Representatives from 1833 to 1844. In that year he was appointed as U.S. minister to Brazil, a post he held until 1847. Returning to Virginia he was eventually elected governor in 1856 and remained in office until 1860. At the outbreak of the war Wise volunteered for military service and was appointed a brigadier general on June 5, 1861. As a general he met with few successes but never lost his desire to fight. Surrendering at Appomattox he resumed his law practice after the war. Wise is buried in Hollywood Cemetery, Richmond, Virginia. Patricia L. Faust, ed. *Historical Times Illustrated Encyclopedia of the Civil War* (New York: Harper & Row, Publishers, 1986) 838-839. [Ed.]

4. This emblem indicated an unwillingness to live under Lincoln's presidency.

5. Wyndham Robertson had been elected to the Council of State in 1830 six years after he was admitted to the Bar. In 1833 he was again elected for a three year term and subsequently was senior member of the council. As lieutenant governor he became governor on the resignation of Littleton Waller Tazewell on March 31, 1836.

6. This cricket club is described in L. Minor Blackford's *Mine Eyes Have Seen the Glory*. Eugene (April 11, 1839-February 4, 1908), like the older Blackfords, was at first strongly for the Union. When Virginia seceded, however, he became a good Confederate. He distinguished himself particularly in the Seven Days fighting around Richmond, at Chancellorsville and at Gettysburg. His served with the 5th Alabama Infantry and by the end of the war he was a lieutenant colonel.

7. Alexander S. Pendleton (September 28, 1840-September 19, 1864) was the son of the Reverend William N. Pendleton, a West Point graduate, Class of 1830, who organized the Rockbridge Artillery, and became chief of artillery of the Army of Northern Virginia. Sandy, as young Pendleton was called, served with distinction on Stonewall Jackson's staff, and was later chief of staff for Jubal Early. He was a lieutenant colonel, not quite 24, when he was killed at Fisher's Hill.

    Young Pendleton, so far as has been found out, always signed himself, "A. S. Pendleton." W. G. Bean, in his splendid biography *Jackson's Man, Sandie Pendleton*, Chapel Hill, 1969, following the example of his mother and sisters, writes, "Sandie." Pendleton was an intimate friend of my father, who, like the rest of his University friends, always wrote it, "Sandy." I choose to follow the example of his college mates.

8. William Barksdale Tabb (September 11, 1840-December 4, 1874) was born in Amelia County, Virginia. He served as assistant adjutant general to Virginia Governor Henry A. Wise in 1861-62 before becoming a major in the 28th Battalion Virginia Heavy Artillery on September 9, 1862. On November 1, 1862, Tabb became colonel of the 59th Virginia Infantry. Wounded in the thigh at Petersburg on June 15, 1864, he survived the war, married Emily Rutherford in 1865, and became a lawyer. Tabb is buried in the Grub Hill Episcopal Church Cemetery, Amelia County. Robert K. Krick. *Lee's Colonels* (Dayton: Morningside House, Inc., 1991) 365.[Ed.]

9. W. Page McCarty came from a Fairfax family notorious for its dueling propensities. In 1873 Page was severely wounded in a duel while his adversary was the last man who died as the result of a duel in Virginia.

10. Robertson wrote in his memoirs that the three of them organized in January 1861. Dr. Philip Alexander Bruce, in his thoroughly documented history of the University, says, "Permission was granted as early as December 5, 1860." He does not say who first suggested the military organization of the students, but Robertson is so definite that he, Tabb, and McCarty started it that I have put the date a month earlier than Robertson recorded it without any notes, to make it agree with Dr. Bruce's statement. Philip Alexander Bruce. *History of the University of Virginia* (New York, 1921) III, 265.

11. Edward Sixtus Hutter, V. M. I. Class of 1859, became a major of artillery. In November 1863 he was a captain in the Bureau of Ordnance stationed at Danville Depot.

12. James Philemon Holcomb (1820-August 22, 1873) was a lawyer and had joined the university's faculty in 1851. As a member of the House of Delegates he signed Virginia's ordinance of secession.

13. The year Frank turned eighteen his father had felt it his duty to go into politics again in an effort to keep Virginia in the Union. In the House of Delegates he opposed secession as long as he could. On March 6, 1860, he was suggesting

that if the Union could no longer contain both New England and the South, New England should carry out her plan to secede, as she had proposed to do at the Hartford Convention forty-five years earlier. In this speech he attacked two bills that he thought would eventually result in the secession of Virginia. "These grave questions have been forced on our attention," he exclaimed, "by a long series of annoyances and wrongs done us by the people, or by the authorities, of the non-slaveholding States, culminating recently in the atrocious outrage on the soil of our State, and on the lives of our citizens at Harpers Ferry."

14. Later Governor Wyndham's brother, Judge John Robertson, was sent to General Scott to ask him to bring his sword to Virginia.

15. Alexander Hugh Holmes Stuart (April 2, 1807-February 13, 1891) had served in the U. S. House of Representatives and as secretary of the interior. At the time of this letter he was doing his best in the Virginia Senate to hold his State in the Union.

16. Williams Carter Wickham (September 21, 1820 - July 23, 1888) was constantly torn between his duties in the Virginia Senate and his duties in the field. Until late in the War he compromised by serving in the Senate when he thought fighting unlikely. As a colonel and as a brigadier general he served under Fitz Lee. He was the grandfather of William Henry Fitzhugh "Rooney" Lee's first wife. In the postwar he was president of the Virginia Central Railroad and also became involved in politics as a Republican.

Early in the hostilities, one cold wet night in bivouac, Col. Wickham said to Capt. Charles M. Blackford: "Blackford, it is a damned shame I should have to suffer so much now and probably be killed tomorrow for a cause of which I do not approve. Remember, Blackford, if I am killed tomorrow, it will be for Virginia, the land of my fathers, and not for this damned secession movement." Susan Leigh Blackford. *Letters From Lee's Army* (New York, 1948) 144.

17. In the Confederate Museum in Richmond is a classic, toga-draped bust of a young man with a beard that carries this label: "James Edward McFarland, Scholar and Diplomat. Done from life in Italy, 1858." When Mason and Slidell were removed by force from the *Trent* in the fall of 1861, McFarland, who was to serve as secretary of the legation to England, was also taken prisoner. He shared the captivity of his superiors in Fort Warren until they were released, and then went on to England with Commissioner Mason.

18. After the War, it was not good form for a Virginian to have any money and an old Confederate had a hard time making a living, but he was proud of himself and he knew his neighbors were proud of him too. The man who remained loyal to the Union, on the other hand, was ostracized at every turn by those who had put their State first, so he had even more difficulty in making an honest living. Alex Rives was one of these. President Grant helped him by making him a federal judge in West Virginia. Alex Rives, Jr., V. M. I. Class of 1856, on the other hand, served under Gen. John B. Hood.

19. L. Minor Blackford. *Mine Eyes Have Seen the Glory* (Cambridge, Massachusetts, 1954) 160.

20. On April 12, 1861, Alexander H. H. Stuart, who has already been mentioned, George Wythe Randolph, an ultra-secessionist, and Ballard Preston, whose views were midway between those of Stuart and Randolph, made up this commission. When they failed in their efforts, all three stood by Virginia.

Chapter 2

1. From the Latin "nolens volens" means "whether willing or not."

2. James Thomas Tosh, V.M.I. Class of 1860, was later assistant adjutant general to Brigadier General Raleigh E. Colston.

3. "The night of April 17, two companies entrained for Harpers Ferry, just after hearing that the Virginia Convention had voted to secede. Indeed the Call for Volunteers had obliterated Union loyalty in both the student body and faculty at the University. The Faculty could not make up their minds to refuse permission, and a leave of absence was granted to all who applied for it. The young men under twenty-one were advised to remain behind; but not even they, it seems, were forbidden to go." Bruce 270-279.

    These student companies remained at Harpers Ferry only four days, April 19-22.

4. William Edmondson Jones (May 9, 1824-June 5, 1864), known both at West Point and in the Confederate Army as "Old Grumble Jones," had been farming near Abingdon when the War broke out. He rose from captain to be brigadier general of cavalry with a reputation as the best outpost officer in the army. However, he did not get along with Stuart and eventually was given a separate command in the Valley. He was killed at the Battle of Piedmont. Jones is buried in the churchyard of Old Glade Spring Presbyterian Church in Washington County, Virginia. Ezra J. Warner. *Generals in Gray* (Baton Rouge: Louisiana State University Press, 1959) 166-167.[Ed.]

5. "Mr. Blackford" was the Governor's son-in-law, William Willis Blackford (March 23, 1831-May 1, 1905). He came under Stuart's eye early in the war and became his engineer officer in June 1862. He remained with Stuart until promoted from captain to major on February 4, 1864. The remainder of his service was with the engineer regiments organized by the army. He eventually became a lieutenant colonel. After the war he was a railroad engineer, a farmer, a professor of mechanics and drawing at Virginia Polytechnic Institute, and an oyster farmer. In regards to his early war service he wrote that he had organized a cavalry troop in Abingdon right after John Brown's raid, and he had asked Jones to head it because of his previous military experience. Jones then spent those crucial early days of the war in Richmond (according to Blackford) trying to get higher rank.

6. Blackford, though, claimed Comet and he gave his note for the figure the Governor had set on the horse. After First Manassas the Governor tore up the note, whether because of Blackford's gallantry that day or because of Comet's does not appear. Comet was wounded in the neck by a piece of shell on September 1, 1862, and was out of the war. Blackford sent him back to the Governor who used him as a work horse at The Meadows.

7. Father and son were together at the time of the Howitzer enlistment, so no letters were written by them about it.

8. In Virginia at that time two towns were known as Salem. This, the older, was where the road from Lynchburg joined the Valley Turnpike going West. It was, in 1861, on the Virginia and Tennessee Railroad from Lynchburg to Abingdon, but there was no railroad Northeast to Lexington. Salem has long since been overshadowed by Roanoke, a rail center next door.

9. John Arthur Campbell (October 3, 1823-June 17, 1886) was a lawyer before the war, but his having attended V. M. I. made him a candidate for a high rank at the beginning of the war. Wounded at Winchester in May 1862, Campbell became discouraged by the promotion of a brigadier general to the brigade he was commanding as a colonel. He resigned on October 16, 1862. Krick. *Lee's Colonels*, 81-82.[Ed.]

10. William Young C. Hannum, V. M. I. Class of 1863, 1st lieutenant and later captain of Company B, 48th Virginia Infantry, was wounded in action and resigned his commission on January 23, 1863. He lived on to 1916.

11. James Cummings Campbell (November 1830-April 1896) was promoted to major on April 21, 1862, but was forced to resign on January 28, 1863, because of a chest wound received at the Battle of McDowell on May 8, 1862. He is buried in Washington County, Virginia. Krick. *Lee's Colonels*, 81.[Ed.]

12. "Camp fever" is hardly a precise diagnosis. The delirium Frank described suggests that he was suffering from typhoid. There are reasons too for suspecting rheumatic fever.

13. Milton White was the captain of the Campbell Guards which was Company B of the 48th Virginia Infantry. He resigned on February 12, 1862. Lee A. Wallace Jr. *A Guide to Virginia Military Organizations 1861-1865* (Lynchburg: H.E. Howard, Inc., 1986) 129.

14. Samuel Vance Fulkerson (October 31, 1822-May 28, 1862) was a lawyer and circuit court judge before the war. He commanded the 37th Virginia Infantry until his death at the battle of Gaines' Mill. It is recorded that Stonewall Jackson regarded Fulkerson highly and cried when he learned of his death. Fulkerson is buried in Abingdon, Virginia. Krick. *Lee's Colonels*, 146. [Ed.]

15. George Wythe Randolph (March 10, 1818-April 3, 1867) was a grandson of Thomas Jefferson. Prior to the war he had served for six years in the navy and attended the University of Virginia. He studied law and began practicing in Albemarle County. In 1850 he became one of the organizers of the Richmond Howitzers, and he was achieving something of a military reputation when he was made secretary of war. Finally, concluding that President Davis was allowing him only to perform the duties of a clerk, he resigned and returned to the practice of law in Richmond.

16. Sam was one of the Robertsons' servants.

17. Gilbert was Blackford's servant.

18. John Pope (March 16, 1822-September 23, 1892) had been brought east after successful campaigns on the upper Mississippi River. He was given command of all the Federal troops in the east except for those with McClellan. Pope's newly christened Army of Virginia pushed south while its commander issued a number of orders which enraged the Confederates. R.E. Lee turned his attention from McClellan to Pope and soundly defeated him at the Battle of Second Manassas on August 29-30, 1862. As a result of the debacle Pope was transferred to the department of the Northwest for the duration of the war. He remained in the army until 1886 when he finally retired. He is buried in Bellefontaine Cemetery, St. Louis, Missouri. Ezra J. Warner. *Generals in Blue* (Baton Rouge: Louisiana State University Press, 1964) 376-377. [Ed.]

19. Wade Hampton (March 28, 1818-April 11, 1902) had been one of the largest landowners in the South prior to the war. He had been a member of the South Carolina legislature from 1852 to 1861. At the outbreak of the war he raised the Hampton Legion and led it to Virginia in time for the First Battle of Manassas. (A legion is a military organization made up of infantry, cavalry, and artillery.) When the legion was broken into its various components, Hampton commanded infantry, but after his promotion to brigadier general in May 1862 he was transferred to the cavalry (July 1862). He became a major general on August 3, 1863 and eventually replaced Stuart as overall commander of the cavalry. He was commissioned lieutenant general on February 15, 1865. In the postwar he was very active in the political arena, serving as governor of South Carolina and as a U. S. Senator. Hampton is buried in Columbia. Warner. *Generals in Gray*, 122-123.[Ed.]

20. Fitzhugh Lee (November 19, 1835-April 28, 1905) was a nephew of R. E. Lee. He graduated from West Point in 1856. Before the war he fought Indians on

the frontier, being wounded on one occasion, and served as an instructor at the U. S. Military Academy. He resigned his commission and accepted a lieutenancy in the Confederate Army. By August 1861 he was lieutenant colonel of the 1st Virginia Cavalry under Stuart. Promoted to brigadier general on July 24, 1862, he became a major general on August 3, 1863. After the war he entered politics and served as Virginia's governor. Lee lies in Hollywood Cemetery, Richmond. *Ibid.* 178-179.[Ed.]

21. Mary Robertson (April 14, 1834-May 22, 1866), the daughter of Wyndham Robertson and the sister of Frank Smith Robertson, was Blackford's wife. Their son, Landon Carter Blackford, had died on December 17, 1862.

22. "Entre nous" means "between us."

23. Jeremy Francis Gilmer (February 23, 1818-December 1, 1883) graduated from West Point in 1839. He remained with the U.S. Army Engineers until the outbreak of the war when he resigned and offered his services to the Confederacy. He was appointed to the staff of Albert S. Johnston and was wounded at the Battle of Shiloh. He then became the chief engineer of the Department of Northern Virginia and later the chief of the engineer bureau of the Confederate War Department. Gilmer became a major general on August 25, 1863. In the post war he lived in Savannah, Georgia, where he was president of the Savannah Gas and Light Company. He is buried in Laurel Grove Cemetery, Savannah. Warner. *Generals in Gray*, 105.[Ed.]

24. Thomas Randolph Price, Jr. (March 18, 1839-May 7, 1907), after getting his Master's degree at the University of Virginia in 1858, had gone to Germany to study philology. More than a year after the War began he decided his duty was to Virginia. He got home Christmas Eve, 1862. His mother was a cousin of General Stuart's. Price much preferred the comfortable life of a student in Marburg or Berlin to that of a Confederate soldier, even when a staff officer. He was that very rare bird, a young man who came in close personal contact with General Stuart yet actively disliked him. Unfortunately, he kept a diary in which he confided his derogatory opinion of his chief in great detail. The diary was captured and excerpts found their way into the *New York Times*. Price left the staff under a cloud and served the remainder of the war in the engineer department in Richmond. After the war he became one of the leading philologists of his day and was a professor of Greek and Latin at Randolph-Macon College, professor of Greek at the University of Virginia, and head of the English department at Columbia University in New York. Price is buried in Hollywood Cemetery, Richmond. Robert J. Trout. *They Followed the Plume: The Story of J.E.B. Stuart and His Staff* (Mechanicsburg: Stackpole Books, 1993) 224-232. [Ed.]

Chapter 3

1. Charles Reade Collins (December 7, 1836-May 7, 1864) was born in Pennsylvania and graduated from the United States Military Academy with the Class of 1859. He served as a lieutenant of engineers in the U.S. Army until early 1861. His first commission in the Confederate army was as a lieutenant of artillery. He was borrowed from the 15th Virginia Cavalry in Capt. Blackford's absence from illness. After Collins returned to his outfit he was promoted to major and later colonel. He was killed at Todd's Tavern. Collins is buried in St. John's Episcopal Churchyard, King George Court House, Virginia. Krick. *Lee's Colonels*, 96; John Fortier. *15th Virginia Cavalry* (Lynchburg: H.E. Howard, Inc., 1993) 127.[Ed.]

2. That point was important because it was on the direct road from Culpeper Court House to Chancellorsville, and so to Fredericksburg. To the south it also com-

municated with Gordonsville and Orange. To the north was Kelly's Ford, through which one could reach Falmouth. Around this little town were great Federal depots, bursting with supplies of all kinds, supplies so badly needed south of the Rappahannock. Stuart was hoping to raid these depots before long.

3. Captain McTier cannot be further identified.

4. Vespasian Chancellor (November 22, 1838-April 28, 1908) was of the Chancellorsville family that gave their name to the famous Wilderness cross-roads. He was a member of the 9th Virginia Cavalry's Company E and at times served as a scout for Stuart. *Robert K. Krick. 9th Virginia Cavalry* (Lynchburg: H.E. Howard, Inc., 1982) 63; Trout 303.[Ed.]

5. These orders of General Lee have not been found, but General Stuart did say, "By the good management of Captain Collins, the enemy was checked for some time at Germanna." *The War of the Rebellion: The Official Records of the Union and Confederate Armies* (Harrisburg, PA: National Historical Society, 1971) Vol. 25, Part 1, 1046. [Ed.]

6. Robertson later recorded additional information as to the fate of the prisoners from one of the officers taken that day. "A year after, I met Captain McTier, who was one of the captured bridge-builders. He says that as they were marched to the rear, they were brutally beaten, kicked and abused outrageously by the oncoming Yankees. It seems that the couriers sent from the picket line to warn us were captured; and half of Hooker's army marching on Chancellorsville was halted for about two hours by our unsuspecting and much overpowered force of eighty men."

7. Alpheus Starkey Williams (September 20, 1810-December 21, 1878) was commanding the 1st Division of the Twelfth Corps which was given the role of taking Germanna Ford. A graduate of Yale, Williams practiced law in Detroit, Michigan, before the war. He was commissioned as brigadier general of volunteers on August 9, 1861. He had fought in many of the major battles in the East and was considered a competent officer. After the Battle of Chickamauga he was transferred to the Western army. In the post war he entered politics and served in the U.S. Congress. Williams is buried in Elmwood Cemetery, Detroit. Warner. *Generals in Blue*, 233-235.[Ed.]

8. Including the cavalry regiment, Brig. Gen. Thomas H. Ruger, who commanded the brigade in William's Division ordered to take the ford, had less than five thousand men under his command that day, and he had not deployed half of them. Robertson's estimate of "fully five thousand" made more than forty years after the event must stem from information he received a month after the engagement.

9. Henry Warner Slocum (September 24, 1827-April 14, 1894) was a graduate of the United States Military Academy in the Class of 1852. He left the army in 1856 after seeing some service in Florida against the Seminoles. Prior to the war he was a lawyer and politician. When the war began he became the colonel of the 27th New York Infantry and fought with the regiment until promoted to brigadier general on August 9, 1861. He achieved his major general's rank on July 25, 1862. Slocum participated in many of the major battles in the Eastern Theater before being transferred to the West where he finished out the war as commander of the Army of Georgia, technically the left wing of Maj. Gen. William T. Sherman's army. After the war he again practiced law and entered politics, serving in the U.S. Congress. Warner. *Generals in Blue*, 451-453.[Ed.]

10. From the report of Col. Thomas C. Devin. *O.R.* Vol. 25, Part 1, 778. [Ed.]

11. Thomas Howard Ruger (April 2, 1833-June 3, 1907) graduated from West Point in 1854, the same year as Stuart, ranking third in his class. In 1855 he resigned from the army to become a lawyer. When the war began he became the lieutenant colonel of the 3rd Wiscousin Infantry and later its colonel. Commissioned a brigadier general of volunteers to rank from November 29, 1862, he was breveted a major general for his heroism at the Battle of Franklin. He remained in the army after the war and for a time served as superintendent of West Point. He retired as a major general in the regular army. Ruger is buried at West Point. (Gen. Ruger's report of this action is found in *O.R.* Vol. 25, Part 1, 707.) Warner. *Generals in Blue*, 415-416.[Ed.]

12. *O.R.* Vol. 25, Part 1, 707. [Ed.]

13. *Ibid.* 719. [Ed.]

14. *Ibid.* 714. [Ed.]

15. Major John Bigelow, Jr. *The Chancellorsville Campaign* (New Haven, 1910) 196.

Chapter 4.

1. Ambrose Everett Burnside (May 23, 1824-September 13, 1881) graduated from West Point in 1847 just in time for garrison duty during the Mexican War. The remainder of his prewar career was spent in further garrison duty on the frontier until he resigned his commission in 1853. For a time he attempted to manufacture a breech-loading rifle of his own design but soon entered politics where he met with more success. When war erupted he organized the 1st Rhode Island Infantry and later commanded a brigade at 1st Manassas. Promoted to brigadier general he led a successful operation along the coast of North Carolina and was rewarded with a commission as major general in March 1862. After the Battle of Antietam he was appointed to command the Army of the Potomac. His dismal failure at Fredericksburg in December 1862 led to his being replaced by Hooker. Burnside was transferred to the Department of the Ohio. He held Knoxville against Longstreet in the fall of 1863 and afterward returned to fight with the Army of the Potomac until the disastrous Battle of the Crater at Petersburg in July 1864. His lack of initiative contributed much to the debacle, and he resigned in April 1865. Failure on the battlefield did not stop Burnside from enjoying success at the ballot box. He was elected to three terms as Rhode Island's governor followed by seven years in the United States Senate. He is buried in Swan Point Cemetery, Providence, Rhode Island. Warner. *Generals in Blue*, 57-58.[Ed.]

2. As of January 1, 1863, absentees from the army totaled 85,123 according to Hooker's own report dated February 15, 1863. *O.R.* Vol. 25, Part 2, 78. [Ed.]

3. Lt. Col. G. F. R. Henderson *Stonewall Jackson and the American Civil War* (London, 1949) 689. [Ed.]

4. John Sedgwick (September 13, 1813-May 9, 1864), a West Point graduate in the Class of 1837, was well known to many of the officers on the Southern side, having served with them in the pre-war U.S. Army. He was respected by all as a fine soldier. Commissioned a brigadier general on August 31, 1861, Sedgwick fought on the Peninsula and at Sharpsburg. Between the two battles he had been promoted to major general. He was killed instantly by a Confederate sharpshooter during the Battle of Spotsylvania. Sedgwick is buried in Cornwall Hollow, Connecticut. Warner. *Generals in Blue*, 430-431.[Ed.]

5. *O.R.* Vol. 25, Part 1, 171. [Ed.]

6. George Gordon Meade (December 31, 1815-November 6, 1872) was another graduate of the United States Military Academy, Class of 1835, who would gain fame for defeating Robert E. Lee at the Battle of Gettysburg in July 1863. Un-

der Hooker he commanded the V Corps. His war service up to Chancellorsville had included almost every battle of the Army of the Potomac and a severe double wound during the Peninsula Campaign. In the postwar he remained in the army. Meade is buried in Laurel Hill Cemetery, Philadelphia, Pennsylvania. Warner. *Generals in Blue*, 315-317. [Ed.]

Following his graduation from West Point in the Class of 1850 Oliver Otis Howard (November 8, 1830-October 26, 1909) spent a number of years before the war teaching mathematics at the United States Military Academy. When the war came he was elected colonel of the 3rd Maine Infantry. He was promoted to brigadier general on September 3, 1861. The next summer he lost his right arm at the Battle of Seven Pines. Commissioned a major general on November 29, 1862, Howard led a division in the II Corps until he was given command of the XI Corps in March 1863. Although his corps was routed at both Chancellorsville and Gettysburg Howard contributed enough in the latter battle to share in the glory and rewards resulting from the victory. He was appointed to command the IV Corps in the Western theater where he remained until the end of the war. In the postwar he took up the cause of the Negroes and helped establish Howard University. He remained in the army holding various positions including commandant of West Point. He retired in 1894. Howard is buried in Lake View Cemetery, Burlington, Vermont. Warner. *Generals in Blue*, 237-239. [Ed.]

Darius Nash Couch (July 23, 1822-February 12, 1897) attended West Point with the Class of 1846 that included George B. McClellan and "Stonewall" Jackson. After fighting in the Mexican War he resigned his commission in 1855 and went into business with his wife's family. When the war erupted he became colonel of the 7th Massachusetts Infantry but was soon promoted to brigadier general. His health broke and he attempted to resign. Instead he was promoted to major general in July 1862 and given command of a division. In the postwar period he held various appointments in Massachusetts state government. Couch is buried in Taunton, Massachusetts. Warner. *Generals in Blue*, 95-96. [Ed.]

7. Richard Heron Anderson (October 7, 1821-June 26, 1879) graduated from West Point in the Class of 1842, fought in the Mexican War, and rose in rank to be a captain of the 2nd U.S. Dragoons. He resigned from the U.S. Army and received a major's commission in the infantry in the Confederate Army. By the end of July 1862 he was a major general and commanding a division in Longstreet's Corps. He was commissioned a lieutenant general (temporary rank) when Longstreet was wounded in the Wilderness in May 1864 and later commanded a section of the defenses of Richmond. He was the State of South Carolina's phosphate agent after the war. Anderson is buried in Beaufort, South Carolina. Warner. *Generals in Gray*, 8-9. [Ed.]

Jubal Early's (November 3, 1816-March 2, 1894) prewar career included graduating from the United States Military Academy in 1837, participating in the Seminole War, fighting in the Mexican War, and studying and practicing law. He became the colonel of the 24th Virginia Infantry at the beginning of the war but was promoted through the ranks of brigadier general, major general, and finally, to lieutenant general. His military service was dotted with successes and failures, but no one would deny that he was a fighter. In the postwar he remained unreconstructed to the end, fighting his enemies, both blue and gray, in the pages of the Southern Historical Society's publications until his death. Early is buried in Lynchburg, Virginia. Warner. *Generals in Gray*, 79-80. [Ed.]

William Dorsey Pender (February 6, 1834-July 18, 1863), like J. E. B. Stuart, graduated from West Point in 1854. Prior to the war he fought Indians and saw some service on the Pacific coast. When the war broke out he resigned his U.S. Army commission and became colonel of the 3rd North Carolina Infantry. Promotions quickly followed as did wounds, which Pender accumulated with sickening regularity. He became a major general in May 1863, but enjoyed his new rank only briefly. He was mortally wounded at Gettysburg on July 2. Pender is buried in the church yard of Cavalry Church, Tarboro, North Carolina. Warner. *Generals in Gray*, 233-234. [Ed.]

Samuel McGowan (October 9, 1819-August 9, 1897) was a lawyer and politician in his home state of South Carolina before the war, serving for thirteen years in the state house of representatives. He also found time to fight in the Mexican war where he received a commendation for gallantry. At the commencement of the war he was made colonel of the 14th South Carolina Infantry. He was promoted to brigadier general on January 17, 1863. Except for the periods when he was recovering from one of his four wounds McGowan fought in all the major campaigns in the Eastern theater. After the war he again entered politics. He is buried in Long Cane Cemetery, Abbeville, South Carolina. Warner. *Generals in Gray*, 201-202. [Ed.]

Edward Porter Alexander (May 26, 1835-April 28, 1910) graduated from West Point with the Class of 1857. Resigning in May 1861, Alexander was appointed a captain in the Confederate Army. He was instrumental in organizing and training the Confederate Signal Corps in the Eastern theater of the war. However, his true talents lay in the artillery where he eventually reached the rank of brigadier general on February 26, 1864, and command of the artillery of Longstreet's Corps. In the post war he was successful in both his civilian and political careers. Alexander is buried in City Cemetery, Augusta, Georgia. Warner. *Generals in Gray*, 3-4. [Ed.]

8. Heros Von Borcke (July 23, 1835-May 10, 1895), or "Von" as Stuart called him, was born in Ehrenbreitstein, Prussia. Educated in Berlin and Halle, he joined the Cuiraisser Regiment of the Guards and later served in the Brandenburg Regiment of Dragoons as a second lieutenant. His exact reasons for leaving Prussia and coming to the Confederacy are not clear though difficulties between him and his father apparently contributed to his decision.

He applied to the Confederate Commissioner to Great Britain, James Murray Mason, for help in getting to the Confederacy, and feeling that the South could use this huge professional soldier, even though only a lieutenant in his own army, Mason helped arrange his passage and gave him letters of introduction. Before arriving at Nassau, his ship was overhauled by a U. S. naval vessel, and von Borcke destroyed all of his credentials. After a few days lay-over in the Bahamas, a blockade-runner brought him safely to Charleston.

When he landed in South Carolina, he had no identification papers and could not even speak English. The German consul believed his story nevertheless and helped him on his way to Richmond, giving him a letter of introduction to the secretary of war. General George W. Randolph took a liking to him and on May 29, 1862, sent him up to General Stuart. At that time Miss Constance Cary described him as, "A giant in stature, blond and virile, with great curling golden mustaches, and the expression in his wide-open blue eyes of a singularly modest boy." (Mrs. Burton Harrison, *Recollections, Grave and Gay*, p. 130.)

Von Borcke spent his first night at the front as the guest of Col. Fitz Lee of the 1st Virginia Cavalry. The next morning Lee helped him find Gen. Stuart, and by the end of the day (Battle of Seven Pines), the General was glad to make a place for him on his staff. He was severely wounded on June 19, 1863, near Middleburg and never returned to duty with Stuart. On December 20, 1864, he was commissioned a lieutenant colonel and sent on a diplomatic mission to Europe. He returned to Prussia after the collapse of the Confederacy where he reentered the army for a short period before retiring to his inherited estates.

9. *O.R.* Vol. 25, Part 1, 778-779. [Ed.]

10. William Henry Fitzhugh Lee (May 31, 1837-October 15, 1891) was the second son of Gen. R. E. Lee. He was called "Rooney" by his father and others to distinguish him from his first cousin, Fitzhugh Lee. Unlike Fitz, Rooney never went to West Point, but he still became a very fine general of cavalry. He was educated at Harvard and entered the U.S. Army for two years, resigning in 1859 to go into farming. Colonel of the 9th Virginia Cavalry, Lee became a brigadier general on September 15, 1862. He was wounded at the Battle of Brandy Station on June 9, 1863, and later was captured while convalescing. Exchanged in March 1864 he was promoted to major general in April. In the postwar he was a farmer, state senator, and in 1887 was elected to the U.S. Congress. Lee is buried in the Lee mausoleum in Lexington, Virginia. Warner. *Generals in Gray*, 184-185. [Ed.]

11. George Stoneman (August 22, 1822-September 5, 1894) graduated from the United States Military Academy in 1846 with classmates George B. McClellan and "Stonewall" Jackson, known then only as Thomas Jonathan Jackson. He served in the West and in the Mexican War. When the Civil War erupted he became a major on McClellan's staff and when that officer took command of the Army of the Potomac he elevated Stoneman to the command of the cavalry. At the time of Chancellorsville, Stoneman was a major general, but his operations during that campaign were much criticized, and he was replaced. Transferred to the Western theater he eventually commanded the cavalry of the Army of the Ohio until his capture in July 1864. He was exchanged but played no major role in the closing scenes of the war. In the postwar period he entered politics and served four terms as governor of California. Stoneman is buried in Lakewood, New York. Warner. *Generals in Blue*, 481-482. [Ed.]

12. Before the war Ambrose Ranson Wright (April 26, 1826-December 21, 1872) practiced law and became involved in politics in his home state of Georgia. Commissioned colonel of the 3rd Georgia Infantry at the outbreak of the war he served in North Carolina and Georgia until June 1862 when he was promoted to brigadier general and transferred to the Army of Northern Virginia. Wright was seriously wounded at Sharpsburg but recovered and was commissioned major general in November 1864 and assigned to a command in Georgia when he remained until the war's end. He resumed his law practice after the war and entered politics. Wright is buried in City Cemetery, Augusta, Georgia. Warner. *Generals in Gray*, 345-346. [Ed.]

13. Robert Franklin Beckham (May 6, 1837-December 5, 1864) was born in Culpeper, Virginia, and attended West Point, graduating in 1859. Resigning from the U.S. Army in May 1861 he fought in the artillery at First Manassas and then served on the staff of General G. W. Smith as aide-de-camp and ordnance officer. On April 7, 1863 he took command of the Stuart Horse Artillery after the death of John Pelham. He was promoted colonel and transferred to the Western army in February 1864 where he commanded Gen. S. D. Lee's corps artillery. He was mortally wounded at the Battle of Columbia on November 29, 1864. Beckham is buried in St. John's Church Cemetery in Ashwood, Tennessee. Trout 56-62. [Ed.]

14. There were actually six guns from different batteries of the horse artillery present (three from Captain William M. McGregor's battery, two from Captain Marcellus N. Moorman's battery (Lt. Charles R. Phelps' section), and one from Captain James Breathed's battery), but Beckham used only four, keeping two in reserve.

    Though Jackson, Stuart, and staffs retreated, Beckham's four guns held out more than an hour against eight pieces commanded by Lt. C. E. Winegar and Lt. F. B. Crosby, soon joined by two more firing from Hazel Grove.

    It was not quite as bad as Robertson remembered it, though Major Beckham said, "I do not think that men have often been under hotter fire than that to which we were subjected." It is also recorded, "One gun from McGregor's battery, commanded by Lieutenant Robert P. Burwell had every man about it wounded except one." [*O.R.* Vol. 25, Part 1, 1048-1051.] Total losses were 2 killed and six wounded in McGregor's battery. There were no reports for Breathed's or Moorman's batteries though John J. Shoemaker (then a lieutenant in Moorman's battery and later its captain) reported after the war that his battery had five men wounded. [Ed.]

15. Richard Channing Price (February 24, 1842-May 1, 1863) was the brother of Thomas R. Price, Robertson's fellow assistant engineer. Channing had developed the unique talent of almost total auditory memorization while working with his father before the war. Stuart at first attached him to his staff as an aide-de-camp but soon had him promoted to be his adjutant general to take advantage of his ability. Price is buried in Hollywood Cemetery, Richmond, Virginia. Trout 218-224. [Ed.]

16. Talcott Eliason (1826-October 22, 1896) came from a military family, his father, William A. Eliason, having graduated from West Point first in the Class of 1821. He attended medical school in Philadelphia, Pennsylvania, and established his prewar practice in Warrenton, Virginia. He became surgeon for the 1st Virginia Cavalry and by January 1862 was medical director for Stuart's newly formed brigade. He served in this capacity until his health caused him to be relieved. He practiced medicine after the war, first in Upperville near Warrenton and then in Hancock, Maryland. Eliason is buried in the Presbyterian Cemetery in Hancock. Trout 99-102. [Ed.]

17. "in the air" — A military term meaning that the end of a defensive line is not anchored on a natural formation (ie. a hill or river) or a man made feature (ie. a town) which would assist the defense in maintaining its position more easily if attacked. [Ed.]

18. Jedediah Hotchkiss (November 30, 1828-January 17, 1899) became the premier topographical engineer in the Army of North Virginia. He made himself invaluable to Stonewall Jackson, on whose staff he served, and was trusted implicitly by his commander. An educator before the war Hotchkiss taught himself the art of map making and fine-tuned his talent in the Western theater of the war before joining Jackson early in 1862. Following Jackson's death he served under Jubal Early. His postwar years were occupied in education and in the promotion and development of Virginia's natural resources. Faust 370-371. [Ed.]

19. Lafayette McLaws (January 15, 1821-July 24, 1897) graduated from West Point in 1842, the same class as James Longstreet. His prewar career included service in Mexico and duty at various army posts in the south and southwest. He resigned his commission in March 1861 and was soon the colonel of the 10th Georgia Infantry. Promotions in September 1861 and May 1862 elevated him to the rank of major general and divisional command in Longstreet's 1st Corps. A controversy with his old classmate eventually led to McLaws being reassigned

to a command in Georgia where he subsequently served under Joe Johnston until his surrender at Greensboro, North Carolina. After the war McLaws entered the insurance business. He is buried Savannah, Georgia. Warner. *Generals in Gray*, 204-205. [Ed.]

20. Robert Emmett Rodes (March 29, 1829-September 19, 1864) graduated from the Virginia Military Institute in 1848 but accepted an assistant professorship at the school and remained to teach for several years. Upon his resignation he became a civil engineer. When the war commenced he entered the Confederate Army as colonel of the 5th Alabama Infantry. His actions at 1st Manassas earned him the rank of brigadier general in October 1861. A serious wound suffered at Gaines's Mill kept him from his duties for some time but he returned to take part in the Sharpsburg Campaign. Rodes demonstrated his fitness for higher command at Chancellorsville and following that battle he was promoted to major general. After Jackson's death he served under Jubal Early. Rodes was mortally wounded at the Battle of Winchester and was buried in Lynchburg, Virginia. *Ibid.* 263. [Ed.]

21. Isaac Ridgeway Trimble (May 15, 1802-January 2, 1888) served in the U.S. Army for ten years following his graduation from West Point in 1822. After his resignation he worked as an engineer for several railroad companies. At the commencement of the war he became a colonel of engineers in the Virginia state forces. In August 1861 he was promoted to brigadier general and assigned to command a brigade of infantry under R.S. Ewell. Trimble's luck ran out at 2nd Manassas where he was severely wounded and upon his return was again wounded, this time losing a leg, at Gettysburg where he was also taken prisoner. Not exchanged until March 1865 he attempted to rejoined the army but instead heard of its surrender at Appomattox. Trimble is buried in Green Mount Cemetery, Baltimore, Maryland. *Ibid.* 310-311. [Ed.]

Raleigh Edward Colston (October 31, 1825-July 29, 1896) was a Frenchman by birth, emigrating to the United States in 1842 to attend the Virginia Military Institute from which he graduated in 1846. He remained at the institute, teaching a variety of subjects until the outbreak of the war when he became the colonel of the 16th Virginia Infantry. In December 1861 Colston was promoted to the rank of brigadier general and served with the Army of Northern Virginia until after Chancellorsville. His performance there was unsatisfactory and he was transferred south to Beauregard at Petersburg. His post war career included running a military school and accepting a colonelcy in the Egyptian Army. Upon Colston's return to the United States he was reduced to poverty by failed investment. His health broke due to old wounds, and he spent the last two years of his life in the Confederate Soldiers' Home in Richmond, Virginia. He is buried in Hollywood Cemetery in Richmond. *Ibid.* 58-59. [Ed.]

21. Born in Wheeling, Virginia (now West Virginia) Walter Quarrier Hullihen (June 14, 1841-May 8, 1923) was attending the University of Virginia when the war began. He enlisted in the second company of the Richmond Howitzers on May 27, 1861, and served with this unit until he received a cadetship on August 1, 1862, when he was commissioned a second lieutenant and assigned to the Madison Light Artillery. His service with this battery was very brief, and in September he reported to Stuart as a aide-de-camp. He was severely wounded at Chancellorsville and incapacitated for some time. He was promoted to captain on November 19, 1863, and assigned as inspector to Gen. L. L. Lomax's brigade. Hullihen was with Stuart when he was wounded at Yellow Tavern and escorted him to Dr. Charles Brewer's. After the War, he entered the Episcopal ministry and for more than thirty years was rector of Trinity Episcopal Church

in Staunton, Virginia. Much to his discomfiture, his old army friends, including Capt. Charles Grattan, who had been on Stuart's staff with him, continued
to call him "Honey-Bun," as the General had. Hullihen is buried in the churchyard of Trinity Episcopal Church. Trout 179-186. [Ed.]

22. About half of the Eleventh Corps was of German birth or blood.

23. James Henry Drake (June 9, 1822-July 16, 1863) was born in Newtown,
Frederick County, Virginia. He became captain of Company A, 1st Virginia
Cavalry on April 19, 1861. He was killed in action near Shepherdstown soon
after the close of the Gettysburg Campaign. Drake is buried in Old Trinity
Luthern Church Cemetery, Stephens City, Virginia. Robert J. Driver. *1st Vir-
ginia Cavalry* (Lynchburg: H.E. Howard, Inc., 1991) 169. [Ed.]

24. William Woods Averell (November 5, 1832-February 3, 1900) graduated from
the United States Military Academy in the Class of 1855. Garrison duty and
Indian fighting, during which he was wounded, filled his prewar career in the
army. After a short stint on staff duty just after the war's outbreak he was
appointed colonel of the 3rd Pennsylvania Cavalry and commanded a brigade
through the Peninsula and Sharpsburg campaigns before achieving the rank of
brigadier general in September 1862. His entire service was in the Eastern
theater and he ultimately reached the rank of major general. Averell resigned
in May 1865 and pursued a career as a diplomat and inventor until his death.
He is buried in Bath, New York. Warner. *Generals in Blue*, 12-13. [Ed.]

25. When Jackson was wounded, Gen. A. P. Hill succeeded him in command. When
Hill too became disabled, Brigadier General Robert Emmett Rodes, V. M. I.
1848, assumed command. He felt that, since the majority of the troops engaged were infantry and he was the senior general of infantry present, he was
entitled to command. Rodes yielded to Major Sandy Pendleton's message that
Jackson wished Stuart to take charge. *O.R.* Vol. 25, Part 1, 942. [Ed.]

26. *O.R.* Vol. 5, 473-495.

27. Daniel Edgar Sickles (October 20, 1819-May 3,1914) epitomized the political
general of the Civil War period. A politician before the war, he served in the
New York State Senate and in the U.S. House of Representatives. In 1859 he
became the first defendant to plead temporary insanity to a charge of murder.
He was acquitted. When the war commenced he became a brigadier general of
volunteers in September 1861 and a major general in November 1862. A difficult subordinate Sickles nevertheless displayed many attributes of a good commander and was utterly fearless. His tendency to go his own way led to his
corps being roughly handled at Gettysburg when he advanced from the line
Meade intended him to hold. Sickles lost his right leg in the fight that followed
and never commanded troops in combat again. In the postwar he was a diplomat and Congressman. He is buried in Arlington National Cemetery. Warner.
Generals in Blue, 446-447. [Ed.]

Alfred Pleasonton (July 7, 1824-February 17, 1897) was born in Washington, D.C. Graduating from West Point in 1844 he served in the Mexican War
and was brevetted for gallantry. His service also included fighting Indians on
the frontier and the Seminoles in Florida. Pleasonton began his Civil War career as captain of the 2nd Cavalry (formerly the 2nd Dragoons). He became a
brigadier general on July 18, 1862, and a major general on June 22, 1863. With
the coming of U. S. Grant and Philip Sheridan in 1864 Pleasonton was relieved
of command of the cavalry and sent to Department of Missouri for the remainder of the war. After the war he remained in the army until 1888 when he
retired. Pleasonton is buried in the Congressional Cemetery, Washington, D.C.
Ibid. 559-560. [Ed.]

28. James Jay Archer (December 19, 1817-October 24, 1864) studied for the law at the University of Maryland after graduating from Princeton. He gained some military experience fighting as a captain in the volunteers during the Mexican War and after returning to his law practice decided he liked the army life and entered the regular army in 1855 where he remained until the war began. Archer was commissioned colonel of the 5th Texas Infantry on October 2, 1861, and led that regiment until his promotion to brigadier general in September 1862. Captured at Gettysburg Archer's health was severely affected by his long imprisonment. He was exchanged in the summer of 1864 and tried to return to the army. His health broke and he died in Richmond. Archer is buried in Hollywood Cemetery, Richmond. Warner. *Generals in Gray*, 11. [Ed.]

29. James Henry Lane (July 28, 1833-September 21, 1907) Graduated from the Virginia Military Institute in 1854. He returned in 1857 as an instructor at the school before moving on to teach at North Carolina Military Institute until the war began. Lane was made the colonel of the 28th North Carolina Infantry and received three wounds leading that regiment in numerous engagements before he was commissioned brigadier general in November 1862. He remained with the Army of Northern Virginia until it surrendered at Appomattox. He returned to education in the postwar, teaching in a number of different schools including Virginia Polytechnic Institute. Lane is buried in Auburn, Alabama. *Ibid*. 172-173. [Ed.]

30. Edward Lloyd Thomas (March 23, 1825-March 8, 1898) was a plantation owner before the war but did fight in Mexico as a lieutenant in the Newton County Independent Horse from Georgia. With the outbreak of the war Thomas was commissioned a colonel and given command of the 35th Georgia Infantry. He was promoted to brigadier general in November 1862 and fought in every major campaign in the eastern theater until the surrender at Appomattox. After the war he returned to his plantation, but in 1885 he accepted to position in the Indian Bureau from President Cleveland. Thomas in buried in Kiowa, Oklahoma. Warner. *Ibid*. 305-306. [Ed.]

31. Henry Heth (December 16, 1825-September 27, 1899) graduated from West Point in 1847. He spent his entire prewar service on routine frontier duty. After he resigned from the U. S. Army he was commissioned colonel of the 45th Virginia Infantry. He was promoted to brigadier general in January 1862 but did not join the Army of Northern Virginia until February 1863. Heth was commissioned major general in May 1863 and was severely wounded in the head at Gettysburg. He recovered from his wound and returned to the army, surrendering with it at Appomattox. After the war he was in the insurance business. Heth is buried in Hollywood Cemetery, Richmond, Virginia. *Ibid*. 133.

32. Thomas Stuart Garnett (April 19, 1825-May 4, 1863) graduated from the University of Virginia. A physician before the war he had served as a lieutenant in the Mexican War. At the beginning of the war Garnett had been the captain of the 9th Virginia Cavalry's Company "C" before becoming lieutenant colonel of the 48th Virginia Infantry in October 1862. He was killed at the Battle of Chancellorsville. Garnett is buried in Hollywood Cemetery, Richmond, Virginia. Krick. *Lee's Colonels*, 151.

33. This phenomenon of a soldier (or a horse) being knocked over by a shell coming uncomfortably close is also mentioned by von Borcke:

"A solid shot had passed close to my horses back, and the current of air set in motion by its passage had knocked over both horse and rider. Afterwards during the war, I witnessed many similar cases of prostration of men and animals by 'windage.'" Heros von Borcke. *Memoirs of the Confederate War for Independence* (Dayton, Ohio: Morningside House, Inc.) Vol. 1, 58-59. [Ed.]

34. Robertson must be mistaken here. Pender's report of the battle contains no mention of his adjutant being wounded or killed. The same report does name several officers of the brigade who were wounded or killed. It is unlikely that Pender would have failed to mention a member of his staff. The officer may have been one of the regimental adjutants or another officer and Robertson mistook him for Pender's adjutant. *O.R.* Vol. 25, Part 1, 935-937. [Ed.]

35. Although there was plenty of ammunition south of the Rappahannock, its distribution was spotty, due to inefficiency of certain ordnance officers, and to the division of responsibility between quartermasters and ordnance officers. Bigelow, *The Chancellorsville Campaign* pp. 375-378.

   "About this time artillery at Fairview was running out of ammunition,— only canister left which couldn't reach Confederate guns or be fired over Yankee heads." *Ibid*. p. 350.

36. Hilary Pollard Jones (July 13, 1833-1913) rose through the ranks from captain (in February 1862) to colonel (in February 1864). He acted as chief of the artillery of the 2nd Corps after Chancellorsville. At the time of the Battle of Chancellorsville Jones was a lieutenant colonel. Krick. *Lee's Colonels*, 214. [Ed.]

37. Theodore Stanford Garnett (October 28, 1844-April 27, 1915) originally served as clerk and courier at Stuart's headquarters, being detached from Company F, 9th Virginia Cavalry. Robertson and Garnett were undoubtedly together during the Chancellorsville Campaign, but Garnett was not an officer at the time. He received his commission as a lieutenant and aide-de-camp to Stuart on February 17, 1864. After Stuart's death he served on the staff of W. H. F. Lee, becoming a captain on March 1, 1865. He attended the University of Virginia and was a lawyer in the postwar. Garnett is buried in Elmwood Cemetery, Norfolk, Virginia. Trout 132-139. [Ed.]

Chapter 5

1. Sam, Robertson's servant, was still recuperating from pneumonia.

2. The identity of Maj. Peyton is somewhat of a mystery, but two men are possibilities. Maj. Henry E. Peyton was at this time Lee's assistant adjutant and inspector general and may have attended the review as Lee's representative. The other candidate is Maj. Thomas Green Peyton. During Randolph's term as Secretary of War the Conscription Act took effect. Peyton was assigned by Randolph to take command of the men reporting for assignment under the regulations of the act. He was from Richmond and may have accompanied Randolph to the review. Since Robertson states that both men came from Richmond Maj. Thomas G. Peyton was probably the officer in question. John C. Shields. "The Old Camp Lee," *Southern Historical Society Papers*, Vol. 26 (1898), 241-246. [Ed.]

3. Buff was the facing color (used on collars and cuffs) of the Confederate Engineer Corps. As a second lieutenant Robertson would have had one row of gold braid on his coat sleeve.

4. Beverly Holcombe Robertson (June 5, 1827-November 12, 1910), no relation to Frank, graduated from West Point in 1849 and served with the 2nd Dragoons until he accepted a commission in the Confederate Army on March 16, 1861. He was elected colonel of the 4th Virginia Cavalry in late 1861 but lost a second election in April 1862. He was promoted to brigadier general on June 9, 1862. Robertson had a poor relationship with Stuart, and eventually he was relieved of his command and sent to South Carolina where he remained until nearly the end of the war. In the postwar he moved to Washington and was engaged in the insurance business. Robertson is buried on Rock Castle Farm in Amelia County, Virginia. Warner. *Generals in Gray*, 259-260. [Ed.]

5. Born in Philadelphia, Henry Brainerd McClellan (October 14, 1840-October 1, 1904) was graduated from Williams College in Massachusetts in 1858 with four degrees. Until the war began he was a tutor in Virginia and when that state left the Union he decided to join the Confederate army. He enlisted in the 3rd Virginia Cavalry and was soon appointed lieutenant and adjutant. Joining Stuart's staff on May 16, 1863, he remained there until Stuart's death. He then served as adjutant on the staffs of R. E. Lee and Wade Hampton. McClellan became the headmaster of the Sayre Female Institute of Lexington, Kentucky, after the war. He is buried in Lexington Cemetery. Trout 197-204. [Ed.]

6. Norman Richard FitzHugh (December 8, 1831-May 13, 1915) had joined Stuart as an adjutant on June 24, 1862. An efficient officer in all respects FitzHugh moved to the quartermaster position on the staff with the resignation of Samuel H. Hairston. Stuart then added McClellan. After Stuart's death FitzHugh served as Wade Hampton's quartermaster until captured on December 1, 1864. He spent the rest of the war in prison. He was an orange grower in Florida in the postwar. FitzHugh is buried in Evergreen Cemetery, Jacksonville, Florida. Trout 114-119. [Ed.]

7. H. B. McClellan. *I Rode with J.E.B. Stuart* (Bloomington: Indiana University Press, 1958) 262.

8. John Brown Gordon (February 6, 1832-January 9, 1904) was educated to be a lawyer but at the time the war erupted was attempting to develop coal mines in Georgia. He was elected captain of an infantry company known as the Raccoon Roughs. His career was one of the most remarkable in the war considering he had no military training. He rose to the rank of lieutenant general and became one of Robert E. Lee's most trusted generals by the end of the war. A poitician in the postwar, he served three terms in the U.S. Senate and one term as governor of Georgia. Gordon became very active in the Confederate Veterans organization and commanded that body from 1890 until his death. He is buried in Oakland Cemetery, Atlanta, Georgia. Warner. *Generals in Gray*, 111. [Ed.]

There were two generals named Terry, Brig. Gen. William Terry (August 14, 1824-September 5, 1888) and Brig. Gen. William Richard Terry (March 12, 1827-March 28, 1897). Both were infantry officers and since their commands were in the Army of Northern Virginia Robertson could have come in contact with either one. *Ibid*. 302-303. [Ed.]

James Dearing (April 25, 1840-April 23, 1865) received his appointment to West Point in 1858 but due to the coming of the war resigned in April 1861 to enter the Confederate Army. Beginning his service as a lieutenant in the artillery Dearing very quickly demonstrated his talent for fighting the big guns. He rose to the rank of major before transferring to the cavalry. On April 29, 1864 he became a brigadier general. He was mortally wounded on April 6, 1865, at High Bridge during the retreat from Richmond. Dearing is buried in Spring Hill Cemetery, Lynchburg, Virginia. *Ibid*. 69-70. [Ed.]

9. Fitz Lee, though with his brigade, was incapacitated with inflammatory rheumatism. The brigade was temporarily commanded by Col. Thomas Taylor Munford (March 28, 1831-February 27, 1918) who graduated from the Virginia Military Institute in 1852. He had been a planter before the war. Stuart had wished to make him a brigadier instead of Jones, but never succeeded in getting Munford promoted to general. After the war he returned to his farming. Munford is buried in Lynchburg, Virginia. Faust 517. [Ed.]

10. James Breathed (December 15, 1838-February 14, 1870) was practicing medicine when the war began. He chose not to continue his profession in the mili-

tary, joining instead the 1st Virginia Cavalry. On April 1, 1862, he became a lieutenant in Pelham's Battery. By the end of the war he was a major. He established his medical practice in Hancock, Maryland, after the war. Breathed is buried in St. Thomas Episcopal Church Cemetery in Hancock. Krick. *Lee's Colonels*, 68.[Ed.]

11. John Buford (March 4, 1826-December 16, 1863) graduated at West Point in 1848 and proved to be a fine cavalry commander. He went on sick leave in November 1863, and he died of typhoid fever on the same day he received his promotion to major general. Buford is buried at West Point. Warner. *Generals in Blue*, 52-53. [Ed.]

12. David McMurtrie Gregg (April 10, 1833-August 7, 1916) graduated from West Point in 1856. He became a brigadier in November 1862 and a major general in 1864. He served in the West the last winter of the War. After the war he was a farmer until appointed United States consul at Prague in 1874 where he served only a short time. Gregg is buried in Charles Evans Cemetery, Reading, Pennsylvania. *Ibid*. 187-188. [Ed.]

13. Hugh Judson Kilpatrick (January 14, 1836-December 4, 1881) graduated from West Point in 1861. During the war he was repeatedly cited for bravery. He led a raid on Richmond in March 1864, and then commanded Sherman's cavalry in the West. He was wounded at Resaca, and he wound up the War as a major general. His postwar career included being the Chilean minister twice and running for Congress twice. Kilpatrick is buried at West Point. *Ibid*. 266-267. [Ed.]

14. Alfred Napoleon Alexander Duffie (May 1, 1835-November 8, 1880) was born in Paris, the son of a French count. He attended the military college of St. Cyr, graduating in 1854. Afterward he served in Algiers, Senagal, the Crimea (where he was wounded and decorated), and in Italy at the Battle of Solferino (where he was again wounded). At the outbreak of the war in America he resigned his commission in the French army and offered his services to the United States. He started as a captain and rose steadily through the ranks becoming a brigadier general on June 23, 1863. He was captured by partisans near Bunker Hill, Virginia, in 1864 and remained a prisoner until February 1865. After the War he was rewarded with citizenship and a job as consul in Cadiz, Spain, where he died. Duffie is buried in Fountain cemetery, West New Brighton, Staten Island, New York. *Ibid*. 2131-132. [Ed.]

15. "General Stuart in writing his report of this battle, sent for me to repeat an order which he had given me early that morning." (Robertson) Stuart himself wrote, "I also sent Ass't Engineer F. S. Robertson to Brandy to attend to posting the dismounted battalion, which could not be found." *O.R.* Vol. 27, Part 2, 680. [Ed.]

16. Major McClellan was alone on the hill except for three or four men and one artillery piece from Capt. Roger Preston Chew's Battery under the command of Lt. John W. "Tuck" Carter. The gun had been withdrawn from the action near the church because it had fired all of its ammunition except for a few defective shells. McClellan ordered Carter to fire his remaining rounds slowly, and the lone gun did so well that the Yanks were convinced the hill was thick with Rebels. The Federal troops therefore hesitated long enough to saturate the hill with shells, and so some of the hard riding Confederate cavalry were able to beat them to the elevation. [Ed.]

17. Chiswell Dabney (June 25, 1844-April 28, 1923) was born at his father's plantation, Vaucluse, in Campbell Co., Virginia. Like Robertson he was in attendance at the University of Virginia when the war began. Joining Stuart's staff

in January 1862, Dabney served as a aide-de-camp until November 1863 when he was promoted to captain and assigned as inspector to Brig. Gen. James B. Gordon's cavalry brigade. After Gordon's death in May 1864, he served on the staff of Brig. Gen. Rufus Barringer. Dabney was a lawyer and an Episcopal priest in the postwar. He is buried in Chatham Cemetery, Chatham, Virginia. Trout 94-99. [Ed.]

18. Pierce Manning Butler Young (November 15, 1836-July 6, 1896) was born in South Carolina but at an early age moved to Georgia. He attended Georgia Military Institute and West Point which he left before graduating due to his state's secession. Joining the army as a lieutenant of artillery he rose to the rank of lieutenant colonel and command of the cavalry of Cobb's Legion. Promoted to brigadier general on September 28, 1863, and major general on December 30, 1864, Young proved to be a excellent cavalry officer. He became active in politics after the war serving in the U. S. Congress from 1868 to 1875. Additionally he held several diplomatic posts under different presidents. Young is buried in Oak Hill Cemetery, Cartersville, Georgia. Warner. *Generals in Gray*, 348. [Ed.]

19. The Federals lost 936 officers and men, of whom 486 were prisoners. Stuart's total loss was 523 officers and men.

20. Born in South Carolina, William Downs Farley (December 19, 1835-June 9, 1863) was a graduate of the University of Virginia. He joined Company E, 1st South Carolina Infantry on May 20, 1861, and served in that unit for six months when his enlistment expired. He joined Stuart in May 1862 and became part of the staff although without a formal commission or position. His mortal wound at Brandy Station was caused by an artillery shot that severed his leg near the knee, passed through his horse, and removed the ankle of Col. Matthew C. Butler. Farley is buried in Fairview Cemetery, Culpeper, Virginia. Trout 106-114. [Ed.]

21. Benjamin Stephen White (March 11, 1828-March 21, 1891) of Montgomery Co., Maryland, was a merchant before the war. He first came to Stuart's attention during the Chambersburg Raid when he served as a guide. After the raid he was attached to the staff. Though wounded severely at Brandy Station he accompanied the cavalry through the Gettysburg Campaign but then was forced to take a furlough. He never again served actively with Stuart though he was not dismissed from the staff. He ran a horse reclamation center in the Tye River Valley for the remainder of the war. For a time he lived and worked in Baltimore after the war before retiring to Montgomery Co. White is buried in Monocacy Cemetery, Beallsville, Maryland. *Ibid*. 280-283. [Ed.]

22. Robert Henry Goldsborough (January 15, 1841-April 6, 1865) was from Talbot Co., Maryland. His first enlistment was with the 39th Battalion Virginia Cavalry, and he had just joined the staff two weeks earlier. His youth and inexperience undoubtedly led to his capture. Goldsborough might have remained a prisoner for the remainder of the war, but his health broke and he was exchanged in February 1865. By the beginning of April he had regained his health and took a position on the staff of Gen. G. W. Custis Lee. During the battle of Sayler's Creek he was mortally wounded by a shell fragment. Goldsborough is buried in the family cemetery at "Ashby" in Talbot County, Maryland. *Ibid*. 145-149. [Ed.]

23. Douglas Southall Freeman, who had access to Robertson's memoirs, disputes their accuracy (*Lee's Lieutenants*, III, 9. [Ed.]): "In his MS memoirs, Robertson wrote (p. 18), that Stuart said, 'Go, go fast to General Hampton and tell him to send a regiment at a gallop,' but Stuart's contemporary report (*O.R.*, Vol. 27,

part 2, 681. [Ed.]) stated that the first call was for two regiments from Jones. It is quite possible that Robertson carried both messages, and in writing of them many years later confused the incidents."

I [F. R. Reade] cannot accept this. In the first place, according to the reference cited by Dr. Freeman, Stuart himself said, "Ordering more artillery to that point and directing General Jones to send two regiments without delay, I repaired in person to that point.... and then sent an order to Hampton and Beverly Robertson to move up their brigades." (Italics this editor's [Reade]). The discovery of Frank Robertson's letter written three days after the battle establishes the accuracy of his memory in this detail.

Further, Col. P. M. B. Young, commanding Cobb's Legion, reported: "About 12 a.m. I received information through one of General Stuart's aides, that his headquarters were in great danger of being captured by a large body of the enemy which had gotten in the rear. I immediately moved up in the direction of General Stuart's headquarters, when General Hampton ordered me to move forward at a gallop.... I swept the hill clear of the enemy, he being scattered and entirely routed. I do claim that this was the turning point of the day in this portion of the field, for in less than a minute's time the battery would have been upon the hill, and I leave it to those whose province it is to judge what would have been the result had the battery gained its destination." *O.R.*, Vol. 27, part 2, 732. [Ed.]

In short, Stuart, who had been with Jones most of the morning in the vicinity of St. James' Church, "directed" him to send two regiments, and then "sent" an order by Frank Robertson "to Hampton," exactly as Frank Robertson said he did.

24. *O.R.*, Vol. 27, part 2, 734. [Ed.]
25. This was Lt. Carter's lone gun with its few defective shells. [Ed.]
26. Regrettably, when Captain Robertson sat down in his old age to record his adventures, he was not infallible. General Stuart noted of this engagement in his official report: "Before the commands had reached Fleetwood heights, where I had encamped the night before, I received notice from General Robertson's pickets at Kelly's Ford, that the enemy was crossing infantry with some cavalry at that point, two regiments being over already. I therefore sent Colonel [John L.] Black's First South Carolina Cavalry, of Hampton's Brigade, down that road, to hold the enemy in check till Robertson's brigade could relieve him." Stuart, *O.R.* Vol. 27, part 2, 680. [Ed.]
27. Colonel P. M. B. Young, as we have already read in Frank's letter to his sister, led Cobb's Legion.
28. Col. Asher Waterman Harman's 12th Virginia Cavalry and Lt. Col. Eligah Viers White's 35th Virginia Cavalry were the first two regiments of Jones' Brigade to reach Fleetwood Hill. They were followed by the 6th Virginia Cavalry, also of Jones' Brigade, Major Cabell Edward Flournoy commanding. This regiment had begun its day by saving the guns in front of St. James' Church from Buford's men when they crossed the Rappahannock at dawn; now attached to Hampton, this regiment would distinguish itself again in the next hour, though it could muster only 200 sabres. Colonel Asher Waterman Harmon's 12th Virginia Cavalry and Major Elijah Viers White's 35th Virginia Battalion quickly followed. Stuart, *O.R.* Vol. 27, part 2, 681. [Ed.]
29. Robertson wrote these memoirs after the age of flight was fairly well established. [Ed.]
30. Lunsford Lindsay Lomax (November 4, 1835-May 28, 1913) graduated from the United States Military Academy in the Class of 1856. During his short

period of service in the U.S. Army he was stationed with the cavalry on frontier duty. He resigned his commission in April 1861 and immediately joined the Virginia State forces as a captain. A staff officer until 1863 Lomax was promoted to colonel and assigned to the 11th Virginia Cavalry. By summer of that year he was a brigadier general. In August 1864 he was commissioned major general and for much of the remainder of that year he fought in the Shenandoah Valley under Jubal Early. He surrendered his command in Greensboro, North Carolina. In the postwar he was president of Virginia Polytechnic Institute and commissioner of Gettysburg National Military Park. Lomax is buried in Warrenton, Virginia. Warner. *Generals in Gray*, 190-191. [Ed.]

31. John Randolph Chambliss, Jr. (January 23, 1833-August 16, 1864) was a Virginian and a graduate of the United States Military Academy in the class of 1853. He resigned his army commission in 1854 to become a planter. At the war's beginning he was commissioned a colonel in the 41st Virginia Infantry, a position he held for only a short time. In July 1861 he was appointed colonel of the 13th Virginia Cavalry, where he remained until becoming a brigadier general on December 19, 1863. He was killed in action during a cavalry battle on the Charles City Road outside of Richmond. Chambliss is buried in Emporia, Virginia. Warner. *Generals in Gray*, 46-47. [Ed.]

32. James Lucius Davis (January 25, 1816-May 11, 1871) graduated from West Point in 1833. After serving with the 46th Virginia Infantry he became colonel of the 10th Virginia Cavalry on September 24, 1862. Col. Davis was not killed at Hagerstown but was wounded and taken prisoner during the fighting there on July 6, 1863. He was eventually exchanged and served until almost the end of the war. He was a superintendent of schools in the postwar. Davis is buried in Emanuel Episcopal Church Cemetery in Henrico County, Virginia. Robert J. Driver. *10th Virginia Cavalry* (Lynchburg: H.E. Howard, Inc., 1992) 107-108. [Ed.]

33. This was not quite true. Pleasonton had 10,961 men, of whom all, except one brigade of infantry, were engaged. Stuart had 9,536 sabres, five brigades, twenty-one regiments; most of Fitz Lee's and all of Robertson's brigades were not engaged. Pleasonton got no information about Lee's proposed movements, and he did not defeat Stuart. [Ed.]

34. Blackford, *Letters from Lee's Army*, 175. [Ed.]

Chapter 6

1. "A pressed guide needs a word to explain. He is any man we may find, awake or asleep, who is a native of an unknown land through which we are passing. Two cavalrymen guard him with drawn sabres; the three head the column. His guards are instructed in his presence to kill him should he show any signs of treachery or guide us wrong." *F. S. Robertson*

2. Duffie's report of this action appears in *O.R.* Vol. 27, part 1, 962-964. [Ed.]

3. There are several accounts of this wounding. Major McClellan wrote merely: "During this movement, Major Heros von Borcke, an officer of the Prussian staff, who was serving on Stuart's staff, received a severe wound which disabled him for future service." McClellan 307. [Ed.]

    The victim himself wrote: "The General was riding a few steps before me on my left—'General, those Yankees are giving it rather hotly to me on your account,'—when I suddenly felt a severe dull blow, as though somebody had struck me with his fist on my neck, fiery sparks glittered before my eyes, and a tremendous weight seemed to drag me from my horse." He lost consciousness when hit. Coming to and "managing to regain my legs with the assistance of

Captain Blackford and Lieutenant Robertson of our Staff, I mounted my horse and rode off the field supported by these two officers, whose devoted friendship could not have been proved by a more signal act of self-sacrifice." von Borcke. Vol. II, 293-294. [Ed.]

Capt. W. W. Blackford "heard a thump very much like someone had struck a barrel a violent blow with a stick...I spurred Magic alongside instantly, and, leaning over, took his foot in both hands, and threw it over, clear of the saddle. His foot fell to the ground and this jerked loose his hold on the mane, letting him down easily on his back. Frank Robertson and myself sprang down to the ground while someone caught his horse.... When we first lifted him up von Borcke was limp as a rag, but to our great surprise and pleasure, he then showed signs of returning consciousness and stiffened himself on his legs enough for us to lift one foot to the stirrup, and then with a mighty effort to hoist him to the saddle, where with assistance on both sides he kept his balance until we would get him to an ambulance." W. W. Blackford. *War Years with Jeb Stuart* (New York: Charles Scribner's Sons, 1945) 218-219. [Ed.]

General Stuart's account: "In withdrawing, while riding at my side, the brave and heroic Major von Borcke received a very severe, and it was thought fatal, wound in the neck from one of the enemy's sharp shooters, who from a stone fence a few hundred yards off poured a tempest of bullets over us." O.R. Vol. 27, part 2, 690. [Ed.]

4.   Stuart's visit is described only by von Borcke who wrote: "At last Stuart himself came,and bending over me, kissed my forehead, and I felt two tears drop upon my cheek as I heard him say, 'Poor fellow, your fate is a sad one, and it was for me you received this mortal wounds.'" von Borcke 296. [Ed.]

5.   Justus Scheibert (May 16, 1831-1904) was born in Stettin and had served in the engineer corps in the Prussian army. In 1863 he was sent by the Prussian War Ministry to observe the American war. He spent time with various generals and their staffs including R. E. Lee, James Longstreet, and Stuart. He returned to Prussia and participated in the campaigns of 1866 and 1870. He retired in 1877 becoming a newspaper publisher and writer of military books and articles. [Ed.]

6.   von Borcke, Vol. II, 300. [Ed.]

7.   *Ibid.* Vol. II, 303. [Ed.]

8.   *Ibid.* Vol. II, 303. [Ed.]

9.   *Ibid.* Vol. II, 305. [Ed.]

10. This Resolution is also published in *O.R.* Vol. 27, Part 2, 712. [Ed.]

11. von Borcke, Vol. II, 307. [Ed.]

12. Von Borcke's courage is above question, but his veracity in the tales of his adventures is not; he has indeed been accused of ascribing to himself heroic deeds of others, and even of gilding some of his own exploits. It is then surprising to read:

"Regularly after dinner, our whole family of officers from the commander down to the youngest lieutenant, used to assemble in the English war correspondent and artist, Vizetelly's tent, squeezing ourselves into his narrow quarters to hear his entertaining narratives, which may possibly have received a little embellishment in the telling." *Ibid.* Vol. I, 317-318. [Ed.]

William Blackford objected to von Borcke's embellishments. He objected particularly to his frequent stories of advising General Stuart, for he felt sure the General neither needed, nor would have put up with advice volunteered by one serving under him; indeed no such officer would have dreamed of offering such advice.

In the closing pages of his book, von Borcke writes stirringly of his attempts to take the field again in the spring of 1864, especially of those on May 11. He was with Stuart several hours before his death, and he gives a dramatic account of the scene.

On President Davis' orders, he sailed from Wilmington, N. C., in December, 1864, finally arriving in England two months later. He was thus spared "the grief of being an eyewitness of the rapid collapse of the Confederacy, and the downfall of a just and noble cause." *Ibid.* Vol. II, 317. [Ed.]

Von Borcke was at the Battle of Koniggratz as a first lieutenant under Prince Frederick Charles. When after a battle he was presented to the famous von Moltke, he was asked, *"Are you not the American?"* That pleased him. He was retired from the German army as a captain. He served later, however, as personal adjutant to Field Marshal Prince Frederick Charles, 1875-'80.

At his father's death, von Borcke inherited the ancestral castle at Geisenbridge, in East Prussia. When Capt. William Gordon McCabe visited him there, he ran up the German flag on one tower, the Confederate flag on the other. Captain McCabe thought at the time it was probably the only place in the world the Stars and Bars might be flown with impunity.

In 1883, Col. Charles S. Venable, recently of Lee's staff, then professor of mathematics at the University of Virginia, on his sabbatical leave took his family to Germany. He got in touch with von Borcke, who invited him to the castle. Venable secured the Prussian's promise to revisit Virginia the following year.

On his arrival in Hoboken on May 30, 1884, von Borcke was greeted by Prof. Thomas Randolph Price of Columbia University, the diary-writing son of Von's host for so many months, who escorted him to Baltimore. There he was entertained by Gen. Wade Hampton, Gen. Rooney Lee, Gen. Bradley T. Johnson, Gen. R. S. Andrews, Col. Stuart Symington, recently of Pickett's staff, Gen. Charles Marshall, recently of Lee's staff, and Lt. Col. William W. Blackford.

When von Borcke returned he had gained about two hundred pounds above his fighting weight, but he had lost none of his exuberant charm, even if he had not been able to tie his own shoe laces in ten years. In his book, Blackford said, "When I met him on this occasion, he threw his arms around me and his eyes filled with tears." Blackford, *War Years with Jeb Stuart*, 220. [Ed.]

Von Borcke went on to Richmond where a more formal banquet was given in his honor. General Wickham claimed that von Borcke "was ever in the front rank of the charge and always in the rear of the retreat. No man in the Confederate Army did more faithful service than Heros von Borcke!"

The Prussian's great Damascus sword, carefully treasured over the years by the Price family, was produced. He was asked to give it to the State of Virginia. This he gladly and graciously did, and the sabre is now on display in the Confederate Museum of Richmond.

True to his promise to his old commander, he paid his respects to Mrs. Stuart, principal of the Virginia Female Institute (after her death, renamed Stuart Hall) in Staunton, and met the General's daughter Virginia. He sailed for home August 15, 1884.

13. "Pleasonton, with a superior force at his command, caused Stuart to retire over a distance certainly not greater than six miles, between eight o'clock in the morning and dark, on one of the longest days of the year...and his withdrawal from one position to another was executed in uniformly good order." McClellan, 313. [Ed.]

14. Confederate losses from O.R. Vol. 27, Part 2, 691; Federal losses from *O.R.* Vol. 27, Part 1, 193. [Ed.]

15. For Stuart's orders from Lee through Longstreet see *O.R.* Vol. 27, Part 3, 913-915, 923. [Ed.]

16. Albert Gallatin Jenkins (November 10, 1830-May 21, 1864) was born in Cabell County in what is now West Virginia. Graduating from Harvard in 1850 he established a law practice in Charleston, (West) Virginia. He was elected to the U. S. Congress in 1856 but resigned his seat in April 1861. As colonel of the 8th Virginia Cavalry Jenkins earned a reputation as an independent commander. He received his appointment as a brigadier general on August 5, 1862 and was elected to the First Confederate Congress at about the same time. Wounded at Gettysburg, he recovered only to be mortally wounded on May 9, 1864, at Cloyd's Mountain. Jenkins is buried in Spring Hill Cemetery, Huntington, West Virginia. Warner. *Generals in Gray*, 154-155. [Ed.]

17. John Daniel Imboden (February 16, 1823-August 15, 1895) had been a lawyer in Staunton, Virginia, before the war and had represented his district in the state legislature twice. His first Confederate service was as captain of the Staunton Artillery. Later he organized what became the 62nd Virginia, a mounted infantry regiment. His promotion to brigadier general came on June 28, 1863. Striken with typhoid in the fall of 1864, Imboden served the remainder of the war as a prisoner of war facility in Aiken, South Carolina. He returned to his law practice after the war. Imboden is buried in Hollywood Cemetery, Richmond, Virginia. Warner. *Generals in Gray*, 147. [Ed.]

18. They spent the night of the 25th near Buckland Mills and that of the 26th in the vicinity of Wolf Run Shoals on Occoquan Creek. They crossed the Potomac the night of June 27-28. *O.R.* Vol. 27, Part 2, 692-693. [Ed.]

19. Note of this engagement has not been encountered elsewhere.

20. Knight's report of the action is found in *O.R.* Vol. 27, Part 2, 201-203; Stuart's account appears in *Ibid.* 695. [Ed.]

21. See *O.R.* Vol. 27, Part 1, 986-987 for Kilpatrick's report; and *O.R.* Vol. 27, Part 2, 695-696 for Stuart's. [Ed.]

22. Andrew Reid Venable (December 2, 1832-October 15, 1909) was one of Stuart's adjutants. A native of Prince Edward Co., Virginia, Venable graduated from Hampden-Sydney College in 1852. From 1856 to 1861 he worked in the merchantile business in St. Louis. It was there he first met Stuart. With the coming of the war Venable joined the 3rd Richmond Howitzers but soon received a captain's commission in the commissary department. He again met Stuart on the battlefield of Chancellorsville where he made such an impression that Stuart asked for his appointment as major and assistant adjutant general to replace Channing Price who had been killed in the battle. Venable served with Stuart until the general was killed. Captured on October 27, 1864, at the Battle of Hatcher's Rum, he escaped through a train window while near Philadelphia and made his way south though not before marrying his fiance in Philadelphia. He practiced farming after the war. He is buried in College Cemetery, Hampden-Sidney, Virginia. Trout 268-273. [Ed.]

23. Henry C. Lee was an aide-de-camp for Maj. Gen. Fitzhugh Lee. [Ed.]

24. William Farrar Smith (February 17, 1824-February 28, 1903) graduated from West Point in 1845, ranking fourth in his class which led to his assignment to the Corps of Engineers. His prewar service included some time as an instructor at his Alma Mater. With the commencement of the war he became colonel of the 3rd Vermont Infantry and fought at 1st Manassas. He was promoted to brigadier general in August 1861. Smith participated in a number of the early campaigns in the Eastern theater until after the Battle of Fredericksburg when

he wrote a letter to Lincoln criticizing his commander, Ambrose Burnside. This, plus his close friendship with Maj. Gen. George B. McClellan led to Smith's assignment to secondary theaters of the war and to the loss of his promotion to major general which was not confirmed by the Senate. Transferred to the West after the Gettysburg Campaign, Smith earned praise from Maj. Gen. William T. Sherman which resulted in his promotion to major general in March 1864. He was then transferred East to fight with the Army of the Potomac under Meade and Grant. His irascibility toward his superiors, Meade in particular, his failing health, and poor performance around Petersburg led to his being relieved of command of the XVIII Corps. Smith held no further commands during the war and resigned from the army entirely in 1867. He was involved in various business ventures in the postwar period. Smith is buried in Arlington National Cemetery. Warner. *Generals in Blue*, 462-464. [Ed.]

25. Smith's report is in *O.R.* Vol. 27, Part 2, 220-221; Stuart's is in *Ibid.* 696-697. [Ed.]
26. McClellan 332. [Ed.]
27. *O.R.* Vol. 27, Part 2, 697. [Ed.]
28. *Ibid.* 699. [Ed.]
29. *O.R.* Vol. 27, Part 2, 724. [Ed.]
30. Like many other soldiers before his day, as well as since, Robertson always tended to exaggerate the enemy's numbers. At the beginning of the battle on the 1st, Lee's army outnumbered Meade's, but the disparity had been pretty well evened up by that evening. The Federal Sixth Army Corps joined Meade on the 2nd, and Meade was able to summon many more to his standards, while Lee was not. Thomas L. Livermore in his book, *Numbers and Losses in the Civil War in America 1861-65*, gives the size of the Federal army as 88,289 and the Confederate army as 75,000.
31. Laurence Simmons Baker (May 15, 1830-April 10, 1907) graduated from the United States Military Academy in 1851. From that time until the beginning of the war he was on frontier duty with the regiment of Mounted Rifles. When the war erupted he resigned from the army and was appointed lieutenant colonel of the 1st North Carolina Cavalry. In the spring of 1862 he was elected the regiment's colonel. Baker participated in all the campaigns of the army and was rewarded with a brigadier general's commission in July 1863. Wounded on several occasions he was somewhat incapacitated for field command and in 1864 was assigned to the Department of North Carolina. He surrendered with Johnston at Greensboro, North Carolina. After the war he engaged in farming and was a railroad station agent. Baker is buried in Cedar Hill Cemetery, Suffolk, Virginia. Warner. *Generals in Gray*, 14-15. [Ed.]
32. *O.R.* Vol. 27, Part 2, 724-725. [Ed.]
33. Vincent A. Witcher (February 16, 1837-December 7, 1912) was a lawyer in Virginia before the war. He became successively Captain, major, and lieutenant of the 34th Virginia Cavalry Battalion. Witcher was a lawyer and farmer in the postwar. Krick. *Lee's Colonels*, 137. [Ed.]

Jenkins was at the time incapacitated with a wound. The brigade was under Colonel Milton J. Ferguson (1833-April 22, 1881), of the 16th Virginia Cavalry. Ferguson was a lawyer before the war and was at first captain of the battalion then colonel of the regiment. He returned to his law practice after the war. Ferguson is buried in Fairview Cemetery, Ft. Gay, West Virginia. *Ibid.* 404; Jack L. Dickinson, *16th Virginia Cavalry* (Lynchburg: H.E. Howard, Inc., 1989) 98. [Ed.]

34. McClellan 341. [Ed.]
35. Here Robertson is guilty of some understatement as the Federal army did mount a pursuit, though granted, Lincoln was not at all pleased with the outcome. Stuart's cavalry was engaged at several places, and for a while it appeared that another major battle might be fought before Lee could retreat across the Potomac. [Ed.]
36. McClellan 364. [Ed.]
37. While Stuart and staff did encamp at the Bower on the night of July 15, Robertson is incorrect at placing the engagement in the preceding paragraph on the same date. The skirmish at Shepherdstown, which claimed the life of Col. James H. Drake of the 1st Virginia Cavalry, occurred on July 16 not on the 15th. Considering Robertson's condition at the time it can be understood if he erred as to the date. [Ed.]
38. Robertson is referring to Major Dabney Ball (May 1820-February 15, 1878), who had been Stuart's commissary officer from October 2, 1861 to July 15, 1862. A Methodist Episcopal minister, Ball was not averse to taking a few shots at the enemy when they came in range, and he established such a reputation as a fighter that Stuart nominated him for a field command. At the time Robertson writes, Ball was not a major (the rank he held on Stuart's staff) but the chaplain of the 5th Virginia Cavalry, a post he would resign on July 19, 1863. He later became the chaplain to the entire cavalry corps under Stuart. He continued in the ministry after the war until his death. Ball is buried in Mt. Olivet Cemetery, Baltimore, Maryland. Trout 49-56. [Ed.]
39. Judge John W. Brockenbrough (1808-1877) was born in Hanover County, Virginia, and moved to Lexington in 1834. President Polk appointed him judge of the U.S. District Court of western Virginia in 1845. He was continued in the same post by the Confederate government. He was a member of the Virginia delegation to the Washington Peace Conference. In August, 1865, he was sent as an emissary of the trustees of Washington College to ask General Lee to become its president.
40. McClellan 394-5. Nobody enjoyed this event more than Blackford, who said, "It was a race like a fox chase for five miles. Next to that after the Lancers near Cold Harbor in the seven days around Richmond, this was the most exciting sport I ever had." Blackford, *War Years with Jeb Stuart*, p. 241. [Ed.]

Chapter 7

1. Gouverneur Kemble Warren (January 8, 1830-August 8, 1882) graduated second in his class from the United States Military Academy in 1850, having been only sixteen when he received his appointment. He divided the prewar years between the engineers and West Point where he served as an instructor in mathematics. At the outbreak of the war Warren was appointed lieutenant colonel of the 5th New York Infantry. Promoted to colonel, he was wounded at Gaines's Mill during the Peninsula Campaign. By August 8, 1863, Warren was a major general and, as chief engineer of the Army of the Potomac, in position to make his greatest contribution to the war at Gettysburg where he played a major role in saving Little Round Top. Following the battle he was temporarily in command of the II Corps before being assigned to the V Corps. His solid, if not spectacular, war record was tarnished when he was unjustly relieved of his command by Maj. Gen. Philip Sheridan at the Battle of Five Forks near the end of the war. Though he remained in the army engineer corps after the war Warren's military career was ruined. In 1879 a court of inquiry exonerated him. Warren is buried in Island Cemetery, Newport, Rhode Island. Warner. *Generals in Blue*, 541-542. [Ed.]

2. Winfield Scott Hancock (February 14, 1824-February 9, 1886) was a West Point graduate in the Class of 1844. Service in Indian Territory, the Mexican War, the Seminole War, the Kansas War, and the campaign against the Mormons in Utah filled his prewar years. When the war began he remained in California and not until the fall of 1861 did he come East. George B. McClellan had him immediately commissioned a brigadier general. A little over a year later, Hancock was a major general in command of a division in the II Corps. Seriously wounded at Gettysburg he did not return to the army until near the end of the year. He fought with the army until November 1864 when his wound again forced him to relinquish command and he never again led troops in the field. He remained in the army in the postwar and ran for president in 1868, losing to James Garfield. Hancock is buried in Montgomery Cemetery, Norristown, Pennsylvania. *Ibid.* 202-204. [Ed.]

3. Bessie Nicholas cannot be further identified. [Ed.]

4. After his wounding at Brandy Station on June 9, 1863, "Rooney" Lee was sent to "Hickory Hill," the home of Brig. Gen. Williams C. Wickham, Lee's father-in-law, near Hanover Court House to recuperate. News of his whereabouts leaked out, and near the end of June a detachment of cavalry was sent by Maj. Gen. Benjamin F. Butler which succeeded in capturing Lee. During the time he was held prisoner his wife died.

5. John Esten Cooke (November 3, 1830-September 27, 1886) served on Stuart's staff longer than any other officer. A well-known author before the war, Cooke became Stuart's voluntary aide in late March 1862. His first permanent position on the staff was that of ordnance officer. In October 1863 Stuart decided to make use of Cooke's talents as a writer and had him transferred to the adjutant general's department. Following Stuart's death Cooke served as and inspector for the horse artillery under Brig. Gen. William N. Pendleton. After the war he tried farming, in which he found little success, and continued his writing. Cooke is buried in Old Chapel Cemetery, Clarke County, Virginia. Trout 89-94. [Ed.]

6. Blackford, *War Years with Jeb Stuart*, 250. [Ed.]

7. James Byron Gordon (November 2, 1822-May 18, 1864) was born in Wilkesboro, North Carolina. Prior to the war he was in the mercantile business and did some farming. He enlisted as a private in the Wilkes Valley Guards but was soon elected lieutenant and eventually captain. He became a major in the 1st North Carolina Cavalry and soon after came under Stuart's command. His commission as a brigadier general was dated September 28, 1863. He was mortally wounded at Meadows Bridge near Richmond the day after Stuart received his mortal wound at Yellow Tavern. Gordon is buried in St. Paul's Episcopal Churchyard, Wilkesboro, North Carolina. Warner. *Generals in Gray*, 110-111. [Ed.]

8. Alfred Landon Rives was the assistant chief engineer under Maj. Gen. Jeremy F. Gilmer. [Ed.]

9. Lt. Col. Blackford's father had died April 14, 1864. [Ed.]

10. Charles Carter Lee was the brother of Robert E. Lee. [Ed.]

11. This was also a rumor. New Berne had fallen to Federal forces in March 1862. The Confederates made an attempt to retake the city in February 1864 but failed. [Ed.]

12. Stuart was mortally wounded by a pistol ball from a .44 caliber Colt revolver fired by Pvt. John A. Huff of the 5th Michigan Cavalry. [Ed.]

13. Dr. John Boursiquot Fontaine (April 1, 1840-October 1, 1864) was the son of Edmund Fontaine, a wealthy railroad entrepreneur. His first war service was

as assistant surgeon with the 4th Virginia Cavalry. Promoted to full surgeon (equivalent to a major) on September 26, 1862, he assumed the position of medical director to the cavalry sometime in October 1863 with the resignation of Talcott Eliason. After Stuart's death Fontaine retained his position and served with Gen. Wade Hampton. He was mortally wounded in the performance of his duties while trying to reach Brig. Gen. John Dunovant in a cavalry fight along the Vaughan Road southwest of Petersburg. He died three hours later. Fontaine rests in the family cemetery near Beaver Dam Station, Virginia. Trout 119-124. [Ed.]

14. This, the simplest account of the General's death, seems to me [F.R. Reade], who have seen brave men die, the most credible. [Editors note: No other account of Stuart's death mentions Robertson's presence. However, this does not mean that he was not there for neither McClellan nor von Borcke mentions the presence of Theodore S. Garnett, Stuart's aide, but he also was present.]

15. Blackford, *War Years with Jeb Stuart*, 253. [Ed.]

16. Capt. Walter K. Martin was Jones's assistant adjutant general. [Ed.]

17. McClellan 321. [Ed.]

18. Lt. Bradshaw Beverley Turner (1841-1910) had first served in the Hanover Artillery and later in the 9th Virginia Cavalry until he was wounded at Centreville in September 1862. In April he transferred to the ordnance department and then to Lee's staff as an aide-de-camp. He was the brother of Thomas Baynton Turner who served on Stuart's staff, also as an aide-de-camp. (Although Robertson called Bradshaw, "Bob," he was the only Turner that could be identified as having served on Rooney Lee's staff.) [Ed.]

19. Lt. Robert E. Lee, Jr. was the third and youngest son of the Army of Northern Virginia's commanding general. [Ed.]

20. Early, commanding the Second Corps, was sent to the Shenandoah Valley by Lee in the hope that he could remove some of the pressure Grant was applying around Richmond and Petersburg. The strategy had worked in early 1862 thanks to Jackson's brilliant campaign. Initially Early had success, but Grant finally sent Gen. Philip Sheridan to command the Federal forces in the Valley, and he defeated Early who at one time had threatened Washington itself. [Ed.]

21. Rufus Barringer (December 2, 1821-February 3, 1893) had been promoted to succeed Brig. Gen. James B. Gordon. A lawyer before the war, Barringer had also served in North Carolina's assembly from 1848 to 1852. His first commission was as a captain in the 1st North Carolina Cavalry. He was appointed a brigadier general on June 1, 1864. After the war he again involved himself in politics as a Republican. Barringer is buried in Charlotte, North Carolina. Warner. *Generals in Gray* 17. [Ed.]

22. Martin Witherspoon Gary (March 25, 1831-April 9, 1881) was a Harvard graduate who became a criminal lawyer in South Carolina before the war. His initial service was as a captain in Hampton's Legion which he eventually commanded as a colonel. He became a brigadier general on May 19, 1864. Refusing to surrender at Appomattox, Gary cut his way through Federal lines and accompanied President Jefferson Davis and the Confederate cabinet on their attempted escape. The last meeting of the cabinet took place in Gary's mother's home in Cokesbury. He entered politics in the postwar and was defeated twice for the U.S. Senate. Gary rests in Cokesbury, South Carolina. Warner. *Ibid.* 102. [Ed.]

23. Philip Pendleton Dandridge (November 5, 1843-January 8, 1921) was Gen. Rooney Lee's assistant adjutant general. His previous service had been with the 9th Virginia Cavalry. He was appointed a lieutenant in the infantry in

March 1865. Lt. Dandridge is buried in Mt. Hebron Cemetery, Winchester, Virginia. Krick. *9th Virginia Cavalry*, 67. [Ed.]

24. The Federal account of this action can be found in *O.R.* Vol. 42, Part 1, 216-221. [Ed.]

25. Captain Pierce was Gen. W. H. F. Lee's ordnance officer. [Ed.]

26. "Aunt Eleanor" was one of the Robertson family's house servants.

27. Matthew Calbraith Butler (March 8, 1836-April 14, 1909) had been a lawyer and member of the South Carolina state legislature before the war. Resigning his seat he accepted a captaincy in the Hampton Legion and rose through the ranks, becoming finally a major general on September 19, 1864. This was not without cost as he lost his right foot at Brandy Station on June 9, 1863. In the post war he served in the U. S. Senate and was commissioned a major general of volunteers during the Spainish-American War. Butler is buried in Willowbrook Cemetery near Edgefield, South Carolina. Warner. *Generals in Gray*, 40-41. [Ed.]

28. Richard Lee Turberville Beale (May 22, 1819-April 21, 1893) would soon be promoted to brigadier general. He was a graduate of Dickinson College and the University of Virginia and was a lawyer and congressman before the war. Starting as a captain in the 9th Virginia Cavalry, he eventually commanded a brigade. In the postwar he again practiced law and was elected to Congress in 1878. Beale is buried at Hickory Hill, Westmoreland County, Virginia. *Ibid*. 20-21. [Ed.]

29. Major George Freaner (January 20, 1831-November 10, 1878) was Hampton's assistant adjutant general. He had served on Stuart's staff as an inspector. A Marylander, Freaner attended Dickinson College but did not graduate. He practiced law in Hagerstown before and after the war. Freaner is buried in Rose Hill Cemetery Hagerstown, Maryland. Trout 128-132. [Ed.]

30. Thomas Lafayette Rosser (October 15, 1836-March 29, 1910) resigned from West Point just two weeks before he would have graduated with the class of 1861. He began the war as an artillery officer but was made colonel of the 5th Virginia Cavalry after being wounded at the Battle of Mechanicsville. He became a brigadier general on September 28, 1863, and a major general on November 1, 1864. After the War Rosser went West, invested in real estate, made more money supervising railroad construction, and at last became chief engineer of the Canadian Pacific. Finally he retired and settled near Charlottesville, Virginia. Rosser is buried in Riverview Cemetery, Charlottesville. Warner. *Generals in Gray*, 264-265. [Ed.]

31. The Gilliam house [known as "Burnt Quarter"] still stands on the battlefield. Two years after the War, Miss Bena married Major John R. Johnston, of Petersburg. The old home contains Miss Bena's piano, a fragment of her harp, several paintings and a scrapbook. In addition, there are half a dozen family portraits which were pretty thoroughly slashed by Yankee sabres on April 1, 1865. The family does not plan to have them sewed up.

On November 29, 1867, a few months after Miss Gilliam married, Rooney Lee, aged 30, married a second time. The bride, Miss Mary Tabb Bolling, of Petersburg, had ten bridesmaids and the groom at least that many attendants, one of whom may have been Frank Robertson.

General Lee settled at Ravensworth in Fairfax County, near the Episcopal High School. He sent his son to school there. I [F. R. Reade] have learned recently that he was at my father's wedding in 1884. Gen. Lee served in the U. S. House of Representatives the last four years of his life.

32. The identity of Col. Moon is unknown and is most likely a transcribing error on F. R. Reade's part. The most likely candidate for the officer referred to by Robertson would be Lt. Col. Roger Moore of the 3rd North Carolina Cavalry. Krick. *Lee's Colonels*, 278. [Ed.]

33. George William Peterkin (March 21, 1841-September 22, 1916) had served as a private in the 21st Virginia Infantry of Stonewall Jackson's Brigade. Promoted successively to corporal, sergeant, and second lieutenant he eventually became adjutant of the regiment. In June 1862 he was assigned to the staff of Gen. William N. Pendleton and served with that officer until the end of the war. He attended the University of Virginia and the Theological Seminary of Virginia and was ordained in June 1869. In 1879 he was consecrated as the first bishop of West Virginia. Bishop Peterkin is buried in Richmond. Editor, "The Last Roll," *Confederate Veteran* Vol. 25, 1917, 419. [Ed.]

34. The Thompson mentioned here is very possibly Pvt. William T. Thompson of Co. G, 13th Virginia Cavalry. He was assigned as a courier for Stuart in January 1863, but his length of service at cavalry headquarters is unknown. Trout 322; Daniel T. Balfour. *13th Virginia Cavalry* (Lynchburg: H.E. Howard, Inc., 1986) 99. [Ed.]

35. Robertson's horse, Lily, had an interesting history. A black mare, Lily of the Valley, the horse's full name, had been presented to J. E. B. Stuart as a gift from his cousin James T. W. Hairston, who served on his staff. Stuart sold the horse to Theodore S. Garnett, his aide, who traded with William W. Blackford for a horse named Brandy. Lily came into Robertson's possession when Blackford gave him the horse to use near the end of the war. [Ed.]

36. The capture of these three guns was corroborated by Captain Theodore S. Garnett in a letter he wrote on April 7, 1905, in response to an article which appeared in the *Richmond Times Dispatch* on March 26, 1905. Garnett was at that time assistant adjutant general for William P. Robert's Brigade of W.H.F. Lee's Division. He not only verified the capture but gave the name of the battery as Battery A, Fifth U.S. Artillery, commanded by Lt. Charles P. Muhlenberg. [Ed.]

37. Robertson had not known that General Lee, his hungry army all but surrounded, had heard suggestions the day before from some of his generals that he should surrender. He had agreed to let Fitz Lee explore to see if there were a place where he could fight his way out. Fitz delayed his expedition until nearly daylight. In spite of the early successes already noted, it was soon apparent to him that the situation was hopeless. Since there had been no official negotiations as to surrender, young Lee and his division slipped off to join Gen. Joseph E. Johnston in North Carolina. (Later he came back and took his medicine.) About 8 o'clock General Lee sent Colonel Charles Venable up to look the ground over. When he returned with the opinion of General John B. Gordon, at that time this bold young Georgian was perhaps Lee's most trusted lieutenant, General Lee realized that there was no alternative to surrender.

38. Lieutenant Colonel Roger Preston Chew (April 9, 1843-March 16, 1921) was the third commander of the Stuart Horse Artillery Battalion. He had attended the Virginia Military Institute before the war, but left it to join the Confederate army. At the age of nineteen he commanded the Ashby Battery of horse artillery organized by the great Gen. Turner Ashby. He became a

major on February 27, 1864, and soon after replaced Beckham as commander of the battalion. His colonelcy was granted him on March 1, 1865. Chew is buried in Zion Episcopal Churchyard in Charles Town, West Virginia. Trout 79-85. [Ed.]

39. This scout was most likely Private Isaac S. Curtis of Company A, 4th Virginia Cavalry. Krick. *9th Virginia Cavalry*, 67. [Ed.]

40. Henry C. Lee was assistant adjutant and inspector general for Col. Thomas T. Munford who had been "promoted" to brigadier general by Fitz Lee. [Ed.]

41. This item and several others have been lifted from a contemporary notebook, which also verifies several items in the memoirs. [Reade did not elaborate further on the notebook. Ed.]

42. Robertson was all by himself except for Miranda. This thoroughbred mare had been foaled at the Meadows about the time Frank was finishing up at Hanover Academy before entering the University of Virginia in the fall of 1859. She had been his principal mount while on Stuart's staff and later on Rooney Lee's. She had carried him through Chancellorsville, many skirmishers and the retreat to Appomattox. Her speed had saved his life time after time. She was more than a horse to Frank Robertson; she was his mainstay and comfort, his constant companion and beloved friend.

43. Champ Ferguson was from Tennessee. His fanaticism against the Federals was allegedly caused by the murder of his three year old son at the hands of Union sympathizers or troops. On October 3, 1864, the day following the Battle of Saltville, Ferguson and some of his men shot unarmed, wounded troopers of the 5th U.S. Colored Cavalry. Within five days he had killed three more wounded men including a white officer. It was for this crime that he was hanged on October 20, 1865. [Ed.]

44. Robertson did achieve the rank of captain before the end of the war. He had his picture taken in his captain's uniform in the yard of the Robertson's Richmond home in March 1865. However, as he mentioned in his memoirs, he lost the uniform at Five Forks and was apparently paroled in his lieutenant's uniform. It is also likely that with the turmoil in Richmond during the last few weeks of the war that his commission was either never approved or did not reach him "officially."

Chapter 8

1. Cousin Lou was Louisa Johnston, who married Daniel Trigg whose brother later married Pocahontas Robertson.

Bibliography

Bigelow Jr., Major John. *The Chancellorsville Campaign*. New Haven: 1910.

Blackford, Gay Robertson. Unpublished Memoirs.

Blackford, L. Minor. *Mine Eyes Have Seen the Glory*. Cambridge, Massachusetts, 1954.

Blackford, Susan Leigh. *Letters From Lee's Army*. New York: Charles Scribner's Sons, 1948.

Blackford, W.W. *War Years With Jeb Stuart*. New York: Charles Scribner's Sons, 1945.

Von Borcke, Heros. *Memoirs of the Confederate War*. Dayton: Morningside House, Inc., 1985.

Bruce, Philip Alexander. *History of the University of Virginia*. New York, 1921.

Davis, Burke. *Jeb Stuart: The Last Cavalier*. New York: Bonanza Books, 1957.

Donald, David, ed. *Divided We Fought, A Pictorial History of the War, 1861-1865*. New York, 1952.

Downey, Fairfax. *Clash of Cavalry, The Battle of Brandy Station*. New York, 1959.

Editor. *Battles and Leaders of the Civil War*. New York: Century Magazine, 1884-1887.

Editor. *Dictionary of American Biography*. 20 Volumes, New York, 1928-1937.

Esposito, Colonel Vincent J. *Atlas to Accompany Steele's American Campaigns*. West Point, 1953.

Freeman, Douglas Southall. *Lee's Lieutenants*. New York: Charles Scribner's Sons, 1942.

_____. *R.E. Lee: A Biography*. New York: Charles Scribner's Sons, 1962.

Harrison, Mrs. Burton. *Recollections Grave and Gay*. New York, 1911.

Hume, Major Edgar Erskine. *Colonel Heros von Borcke: A Famous Prussian Volunteer in the Confederate States Army*. Charlottesville: The Historical Publishing Co., Inc., 1935.

McClellan, H.B. *The Life and Campaigns of Maj. Gen. J. E. B. Stuart*. Richmond, Virginia, 1885.

Meredith, Roy. *The Face of Robert E. Lee in Life and Legend*. New York, 1947.

Thomason, Jr. John W. *Jeb Stuart*. New York: Charles Scribner's Sons, 1930.

U.S. War Department. *The War of the Rebellion: A Compilation of the Official Records of the Union and Confederate Armies* (Washington, D.C.: U.S. Government Printing Office, 1880-1901).

V. M. I. *Register of Former Cadets, Memorial Edition*. Virginia Military Institute, 1957.

Editor's Bibliography

Balfour, Daniel T. *13th Virginia Cavalry*. Lynchburg: H.E. Howard, Inc., 1986.

Boatner III, Mark M. *The Civil War Dictionary*. New York: David McKay Company, Inc., 1959.

Blackford, Susan Leigh. *Letters From Lee's Army*. New York, 1948.

Blackford, W.W. *War Years With Jeb Stuart*. New York: Charles Scribner's Sons, 1945.

Bruce, Philip Alexander. *History of the University of Virginia*. New York, 1921.

Von Borcke, Heros. *Memoirs of the Confederate War*. Dayton: Morningside House, Inc., 1985.

Crute, Jr., Joseph H. *Confederate Staff Officers*. Powhatan: Derwent Books, 1982.

Davis, Burke. *Jeb Stuart: The Last Cavalier*. New York: Bonanza Books, 1957.

Davis (ed.), William C. *The Confederate General*. National Historical Society, 1991.

Downey, Fairfax. *Clash of Cavalry: The Battle of Brandy Station*. New York: David McKay Company, Inc., 1959.

Driver, Robert J., *1st Virginia Cavalry*. Lynchburg: H.E. Howard, Inc., 1991.

_____. *10th Virginia Cavalry*. Lynchburg: H.E. Howard, Inc., 1992.

Faust (ed.), Patricia L. *Encyclopedia of the Civil War*. New York: Harper and Row, Publishers, 1986.

Freeman, Douglas Southall. *Lee's Lieutenants*. New York: Charles Scribner's Sons, 1942.

_____. *R.E. Lee: A Biography*. New York: Charles Scribner's Sons, 1962.

Fortier, John. *15th Virginia Cavalry*. Lynchburg: H.E. Howard, Inc., 1993.

Harrison, Mrs. Burton. *Recollections Grave and Gay*. New York, 1911.

Henderson, Colonel G. F. R. *Stonewall Jackson and the American Civil War*. London: Longmans, Green and Co., 1949.

Krick, Robert K. *Lee's Colonels*. Dayton: Press of Morningside Bookshop, 1991.

_____. *9th Virginia Cavalry*. Lynchburg: H.E. Howard, Inc., 1982.

McClellan, H.B. *I Rode With Jeb Stuart*. Bloomington: Indiana University Press, 1958.

Stiles, Kenneth L. *4th Virginia Cavalry*. Lynchburg: H.E. Howard, Inc., 1985.

Thomas, Emory M. *Bold Dragoon: The Life of J.E.B. Stuart*. New York: Harper and Row, Publishers, 1986.

Thomason, Jr. John W. *Jeb Stuart*. New York: Charles Scribner's Sons, 1930.

Trout, Robert J. *They Followed the Plume: The Story of Jeb Stuart and His Staff*. Mechanicsburg: Stackpole Books, 1993.

U.S. War Department. *The War of the Rebellion: A Compilation of the Official Records of the Union and Confederate Armies* (Washington, D.C.: U.S. Government Printing Office, 1880-1901).

Wallace, Jr. Lee A. *A Guide to Virginia Military Organizations 1861- 1865*. Lynchburg: H.E. Howard, Inc., 1986.

Warner, Ezra J. *Generals in Blue*. Baton Rouge: LSU Press, 1964.

_____. *Generals in Gray*. Baton Rouge: LSU Press, 1959.

Wright, Stuart. *Colonel Heros von Borcke's Journal*. Palaemon Press Ltd, 1981.

Index